OF MARKS
AND MURDER

OF MARKS AND MURDER

JEN WELSH

NEW DEGREE PRESS
COPYRIGHT © 2022 JEN WELSH
All rights reserved.

OF MARKS AND MURDER

ISBN   979-8-88504-093-8 *Paperback*
            979-8-88504-724-1 *Kindle Ebook*
            979-8-88504-203-1 *Ebook*

Dedication

To all the people who refuse to give up on themselves and their dreams and to those who make sure I accomplish mine. Thank you for giving me the support and resources that I needed right on time, then and now.

I promise to pay it forward.

CONTENTS

CHAPTER 1	9
CHAPTER 2	17
CHAPTER 3	23
CHAPTER 4	31
CHAPTER 5	39
CHAPTER 6	45
CHAPTER 7	55
CHAPTER 8	63
CHAPTER 9	73
CHAPTER 10	81
CHAPTER 11	89
CHAPTER 12	97
CHAPTER 13	105
CHAPTER 14	111
CHAPTER 15	119
CHAPTER 16	129
CHAPTER 17	137
CHAPTER 18	145
CHAPTER 19	153
CHAPTER 20	159
CHAPTER 21	167
CHAPTER 22	173
CHAPTER 23	183

CHAPTER 24	191
CHAPTER 25	197
CHAPTER 26	203
CHAPTER 27	209
CHAPTER 28	213
CHAPTER 29	217
CHAPTER 30	223
CHAPTER 31	227
CHAPTER 32	235
ACKNOWLEDGMENTS	239

CHAPTER 1

Olivia Gabriel scraped the bottom of the yogurt cup and tossed it into the trashcan along with the plastic spoon. She curled the T-shirt sleeves onto her shoulders, pulled her long brown hair into a ponytail, and popped the cap off a whiteboard marker, scrawling the daily agenda on the board as she had done every school day for a decade. The words appeared streaked, barely legible.

Time for a new one.

She capped the dying marker and flung it into the trashcan, where it ping-ponged off the yogurt container and settled. She picked up the little book of inspirational quotes and poems and searched for one to share with her fifth graders. As her fingers moved, her mind traveled two days into the future, nerves already on high alert, preparing for the conversation she knew she had to have when Gina returned from her work trip.

It's time.

A dizzy sensation passed over her, and she rested her forehead on the board's cool surface.

I have to end it.

The metallic sound of the school bell interrupted her thoughts. She unrolled her sleeves and straightened her shirt. Students shuffled into the room, and chairs scratched the floor like worries in her mind.

The second bell rang, and Olivia snapped into teacher mode. She turned from the whiteboard to the students and smiled. "Happy last day of school!" She held her place in the dog-eared book while marking attendance on the clipboard. "Perfect attendance today, great job!"

Students cheered. Perfect attendance on the last day meant a prize at lunchtime. She relaxed at their excitement.

Students giggled as they compared notes about what it might be this time. Olivia let the conversation continue longer than usual because she was looking forward to a prize of her own, it being her tenth-year teaching. For years, she admired others who hit this achievement too. Her heart leapt—finally, her turn.

She frowned, feeling suddenly alone. *Who will I call?*

There was no one to join in the celebration.

Only Gina.

As she flipped to the page, a few kids in the last row made eye contact and smiled at each other as if they were sharing an inside joke. She opened the book to give them a chance to settle into the rhythm of class without her interference.

As she read "The Summer Day" by Mary Oliver, one of the students in the last row leaned over and passed something, a picture or a card, to the next student in the row. The object continued moving across and up the rows until it stopped with Isabel in the middle of the classroom. Olivia pretended not to see but continued to observe as she gave directions for students to take out a notebook.

Maybe it was a card, and all the students were signing it?

Olivia's heart beat faster.

One of the administrators must have put them up to this.

When she finished the poem, she cleared her throat and addressed the class, "What is it that *you* plan to do with this precious summer?"

As students wrote responses in their notebooks, Olivia paced the aisles. Questions pounded in her chest. *What do I plan to do this summer?* Her mind went to Gina, to logistics. It was easy to follow routines; there was no resistance to go with the flow and to do what had always been done. A person can continue in that direction forever.

She sighed and rubbed at a sticky spot on one of the desks.

I can't.

How could she know what ripple effect making one change would have on the rest of her life?

Olivia, focus. Today's a big day.

The timer beeped. "Okay, everyone, who wants to share their goals with the class?"

Students raised their hands, and Olivia called on Antonio.

"Can I turn on the fan, Ms. G?"

The old building didn't have air conditioning. When she had asked about it, the administration said the building was too old. The following day, an open cardboard box with a used fan greeted her at the door like a third-string quarterback. *I'm here,* it seemed to say.

Olivia nodded. "But first, tell us one of your goals for the summer."

Antonio stood and said, "Ride at least five rollercoasters," on his way to the fan.

The fan wheezed, spitting dust across the classroom.

"What's one of your goals, Ms. G?" Antonio asked.

Olivia put her hands on her hips where her shirt met her khakis and looked down at the words across her chest, "Film Major" printed in gray across the top of a black and white clapperboard. Her favorite shirt to wear for the last-day-of-school cleaning was now a reminder of an unfinished dream.

"Thank you for asking." She scanned the faces of one of her favorite groups of students, each child waiting to hear what their teacher would strive for during the summer. Almost all the arts programs had been cut from the school in the last few years. Students were encouraged to fall in love with reading or math, not painting or film. Wearing the shirt and sharing her dream with them might show them that they could pursue many different things. "My goal is to submit a film project to a local competition."

Her film career had been nothing more than a hobby and a part-time volunteer gig with the local community college, but maybe this competition would be a chance for a fresh start.

"Woo," they cheered.

"You go, Ms. G," another said.

She smiled. Everyone should have a group of ten and eleven-year-olds in the room when they proclaim a dream.

After lunch and recess, Olivia directed them to put away their belongings. Despite a great morning, the issue of Gina nagged at her mind. The corners of everything that still hung from the walls shriveled. The butcher paper on the bulletin board had faded from royal blue to grayish purple. Books that had once been neatly arranged by color were strewn haphazardly around the room. Everything in the room—like everything, it seemed, in her life right then—was fraying and fading.

She rolled a dry ball of tape in her hands and called the students back to attention.

"We've entered into the Sparkling Classroom Games, a school-wide competition. The classroom that sparkles the brightest will win a final prize. Let the competition begin!"

She didn't tell them their only real competition was their teacher's expectations.

Students hopped out of chairs in an organized dance. They emptied shelves, packed books in boxes, and sprayed desks with Lysol. She turned on instrumental pop music and pulled the big garbage bin into the center of the room. Students tore things from walls and shot paper balls into the basket, mimicking NBA players.

"You going to miss us, Ms. G?" Antonio asked.

Olivia stood with a group of students taking work off the walls, gently removing tape from the back, and stacking them neatly on a desk. The pile reached as high as the top of the computer monitor.

"Of course I'll miss you," she said. "What will I do without inquisitive students like you in my life every day?"

Antonio and the others clapped their hands together over their heads and wiggled their fingers toward Olivia, the gesture the class made when someone used a vocabulary word in an everyday sentence.

Olivia stared out the window. The sun beat down on a row of cars parked along the curb.

"What's on your mind, Ms. G?" Bobby asked.

"I'm just thinking, buddy," she said, peeling a piece of tape from a poster.

Bobby frowned. "Try not to think too much."

Antonio nodded. "Yeah. Sometimes you just have to experience something and not think so much about it. That's what my auntie tells me every time we go on the rollercoasters. I always want to know how it goes upside down and we stay in, or why I'm laughing so hard even though I'm terrified. She's always telling me to stop thinking so much and just enjoy the ride."

"That's very wise. Are you sure you're only eleven?"

Antonio laughed. "I'm mature for my age," he said, standing taller.

"Are you even tall enough to ride the rollercoasters, Ant?" Bobby said in a sarcastic, friendly tone.

"I'm four feet eleven. Almost as tall as she is," Antonio said, pointing to Olivia. He slapped the air as if to say, "Get out of here, Bobby."

"You've got six more inches to go until you're my height, but you're definitely tall enough for the rollercoasters."

"See," Antonio said to Bobby, "I'm tall enough."

The two kids smirked at each other.

A group of students by the window erupted in a fit of laughter, and Olivia remembered the celebration. She smiled as she played through the events in her mind. She would go to the staff meeting, and everyone would act as if nothing was going on. Then the principal would give a speech. Maybe he would say something nice about her dedication and achievements. Maybe he would hand her a card signed by all her students.

Maybe there will be a gift.

Her stomach fluttered. If she got any cash, she would take herself out to a nice dinner, and then maybe invest in a new fan.

The intercom beeped, and Principal Maylor's voice interrupted their cleaning, "Good afternoon, everyone. We hope you're having a great last day of school. Please pause for a brief announcement." He continued with updates about buses and summer reading. Finally, he said, "Don't forget to take everything home with you for the summer. Teachers, remember, after school, we'll meet in the cafeteria. Have a great summer!"

The meeting.
Olivia smiled.
Finally, recognition.

As they waited for the final bell, Isabel had her head down on the desk. Olivia stepped toward the door to get a better angle. Tears rolled down Isabel's cheek. Olivia tiptoed toward her and bent down as to not make a big deal out of it.

Olivia put a hand on Isabel's shoulder. "What's the matter, sweetie?"

Isabel shook her head against her arm.

"It's okay. You can tell me."

Isabel hesitated and then moved her arm. Olivia peeked past Isabel's shoulder. A drawing on a piece of cardstock looked up at her, a self-portrait, their latest project from art class. The crayon streaks outlined a large head with an oversized, lopsided bow.

The students that morning hadn't been passing around a card for Olivia; they had been passing Isabel's art project. Tears of embarrassment streamed down Isabel's cheeks, forming tiny holes in Olivia's heart.

There was an exercise she used to do with students where she would tell a story holding up a square wooden board with a heart drawn on it. She would tell students about instances when she was called names, teased, let down, and for each memory, she would gently hammer a nail into the painted heart. Then she would tell students about the good things—kind words, caring gestures—and pull each nail out of the heart. She'd ask students what they noticed. The astute kids would name the holes left behind by the nails.

Olivia stayed in teacher mode, keeping on her strong teacher face, speaking in her teacher tone. "Oh, Isabel. It will be okay. This drawing is beautiful."

She stood to address the class. One more "be kind to each other" talk would be good for everyone. As she cleared her throat, the final bell rang, and students jumped out of their seats.

"Have a great summer. Don't forget to do your reading," she said as students hurried out the door. In under twenty seconds, the room emptied.

Olivia sighed. Staples dangled from the corners of bulletin boards. Her cheeks were hot. She went to the window for air. Outside, buses pulled away from the curb.

A man with a briefcase beeped his car locked. The Superintendent of Schools.

What is he doing here?

CHAPTER 2

In the cafeteria alongside her colleagues, Olivia awaited the start of the end-of-school-year celebration. The Superintendent of Schools leaned down to adjust the microphone. His briefcase balanced precariously on the side of the podium. Olivia imagined him unzipping the case before making a speech and sliding out an award. Her award. Ten years and recognition.

She crossed her legs and folded her hands on the table. She swallowed down a wave of excitement.

Teachers filed into the room. The baby-faced basketball coach took a seat beside her. "You have something on your elbow there," he said.

Olivia looked down at a sticky patch of purple. "Oh, yuck." She opened her backpack for a tissue. She scraped at the jelly, remnants of the doughnut prize from lunchtime.

"We've all seen worse," he said.

"You're not wrong," she said, smiling.

Over the years, she had seen it all: She wiped vomit from the floor around the trashcan, scraped gum from the backs of chairs and underneath desks, carried bags of putrid clothes to the dumpster when a student had an accident. But it was all worth it to be part of her students' lives.

She checked the rest of her arms for jelly, or any other substances left on the table from the kids' lunch, and returned the tissue to her backpack. She didn't want to miss anything by getting up and looking for a trashcan.

Principal Maylor joined the Superintendent at the podium, and the two men shook hands. They looked out toward the teachers.

Maylor adjusted the microphone and frowned. With a faraway look, he said, "Thank you all for being here. I hate to start the meeting this way, but I'm afraid I've got some bad news, folks."

Murmurs passed through the cafeteria. The basketball coach leaned back and sighed.

Maylor continued, "Due to district-wide budget shortfalls, our school will be closing."

Olivia stared, unbelieving, at the two suited men.

"You've all heard the rumors about our city budget. The Superintendent has had to make some difficult choices…" his words trailed off.

Olivia's heart beat fast, and her whole body stiffened.

The principal continued despite the groans, "After looking at the data and the resources, the school committee announced they'll be closing down five city schools, and we're one of them. Before you start to worry, please know that I'll do anything to support each of you to find a new home at another school if that's what you'd like. We're in this together."

She squeezed her eyes shut. A voice inside her head told her she should have seen this coming. The emails from the union reps and the school committee had piled in her inbox. In the ten years she had been at the school, they said it was a possibility, but it never really happened.

Things changed, of course, every year—the schedules, the curriculum, the dress code for both students and teachers, the school start time and end time, the staff, the class sizes, the bus routes.

But closing the school?

Olivia shivered. She glanced at the coach, and his face mirrored her shock.

Stan, an older, broad-shouldered guy sitting at Olivia's table, said, "What the fuck. Can you assholes actually do this?"

Maylor continued, "We have a rep from the union here to answer all of your questions, and we'll get all of this sorted out."

"Oh no, no," said Miss Patty, who, in her late sixties, was one of the oldest and most beloved teachers in the building. She put her head in her hands, "Oh no, no. You can't close this school."

Olivia's heart ached. The room turned into a cacophony of moans, shouts, curses, and cries. Her arms were heavy, and her chest was tight.

This isn't fair.

Teaching middle school had been the only job she'd had since she graduated. When she graduated without a job, a recruiter for a teaching program told her about the benefits of a career in education.

The only other option she had back then was to contact her uncle Tim, her mother's older brother, and her aunt Margaret, Tim's wife. Both had extensive careers in film. But she felt uncomfortable contacting them since they hadn't talked to her in over a decade. The last time she saw them was at her brother's funeral when she was ten. Tim lunged toward the funeral director, accusing her of incompetence. He shouted, "It's R-O-A-R-K, not R-O-U-R-Q-U-E," and slapped the obituary in the poor woman's face. Margaret stood by Tim's elbow, steadfast and silent.

At a loss for how to get started in the film industry without making pennies, she accepted the recruiter's offer, telling herself she would find a job in film after a year or two. But it never happened.

She picked at a loose thread dangling from her shirt.

What am I supposed to do?

The Superintendent went back to the microphone and asked everyone to be patient with the district office as they navigated these changes. The collective groan grew louder as he picked up his briefcase and headed toward the door. He walked out the door with the principal trailing at his heels.

Back in her classroom, Olivia stacked books into boxes, seesawing between disbelief and brainstorming what to do next.

Her stomach dropped when she thought about starting over at a new school. She didn't like starting over—too many steps. An idea would come to her mind such as, *Maybe it's time to change careers*, but, thinking about the process—learning the landscape of available jobs, getting to know new people, making it happen—she stopped short of doing anything about it.

But now she had to.

There was no other option.

She sat down at the computer and checked her bank account. A decent balance. Six months to a year in savings. More than she ever had, but far from the security she craved. Outside, a car honked. She moved away from the desk, not wanting to think about what would come next. She sprayed disinfectant on a paper towel and wiped down the green bookshelves, painted by a group of students in her second year.

There was so much she loved about teaching: introducing students to books they couldn't put down; field trips to places in their own city where they'd never been; her after-school "from lit to film" club where kids finally agreed with her that the book was indeed better than the movie; reading the short and sweet end-of-the-year note from the student who never said much in class, "Thank you for showing me that some books are actually good and a kid like me can achieve my goals."

As she cleaned her classroom, aware that she was doing it for the last time, she had a thought that surprised her.

Maybe this is a chance to get a fresh start.

She continued cleaning.

The union rep poked his head in the classroom and asked if she wanted to be added to the list of teachers who were open to opportunities at other schools, should they arise.

She had devoted so much time to teaching. Teaching at another school might be a good option. She nodded, "Yes, please add me to the list."

The school might be shuttered, but she could find a position elsewhere.

Right?

She packed boxes of memories into her car and waved goodbye to the familiar brick building. It didn't feel real. Sadness prickled at the corners of her eyes.

I'll figure it out.

But she didn't feel sure.

When she got home, she parked the car and went into the apartment. Surrounded by the chill of stainless-steel appliances, she dropped a pile of mail on the growing stack on the kitchen table.

Maybe I should sort this.

She left it and went into the living room where she sunk into the couch, shoving aside the packages that arrived when Gina was gone. The quiet seeped under her skin and through her bones, and her body ached.

She pulled her laptop out from the crease of the couch and opened her favorite editing software. She scrolled to the footage for the project she was working on and started splicing pieces together. The clips didn't go well together. Didn't flow. *This is some shit,* she thought, closing the laptop. The weight of the day had caught up to her. She fought back tears.

It was Friday night, and Gina would be home by the end of the weekend.

How do you end something without hurting someone? She didn't believe it was possible.

CHAPTER 3

Paint chips gathered underneath her fingernails as she picked off pieces, fleck by fleck, of what was left of the green paint covering the seesaw. Olivia kept her feet planted in the mulch because if she pushed off she would fall right back down again, there being no counterweight ready to take on some of the burden. Independence, at times, was a lonely job, but one that she had gotten used to.

In the park, she began to wake up. On all mornings, but especially on Saturday mornings after a long week at school, it took a thermos full of coffee and a walk to shake off the grogginess.

In the distance, something cried. An infant or a bird. Olivia glanced toward the entrance. A woman came into view carrying a blanketed bundle. "Shh, sweetheart," the woman said, bouncing a baby as she walked.

Olivia yawned and unzipped the bag at her feet. She ran her fingers along the camera's smooth black surface.

"Morning, baby," she said to the camera.

Everyone had things they found to be most precious. To Olivia, it was her RedMagic professional portable cinema camera. She brought it to her eye and recorded five seconds from her spot on the seesaw.

With the deadline for the amateur film contest approaching, it was the perfect day (and the perfect place) to capture footage for her project. She tried not to think about the things back at her apartment that she needed to tend to, deal with. Things like her relationship. Things like her job. Things she'd rather not think about on a gorgeous Saturday morning.

Rhode Island's Woodbridge Park was a favorite among locals. It was no Central Park, but it was large enough. Shaped like a fishhook and heavily forested at its border, Olivia couldn't see the other end of the park from where she sat. Weekend regulars began to fill the paths. Parents pushed babies in bucket swings. Shoeless hippies read in hammocks. Groups of people in sweatbands did coordinated activities. Kids in sports uniforms traipsed through the dirt.

Olivia, camera dangling around her neck, prepared to capture footage for the contest. She brushed her hands off on her jeans and pulled the contest flyer out of her pocket. The sun crept up above the trees.

She reread the flyer from top to bottom.

Providence Amateur Film Contest

Calling entries for short films for World Mental Health Day. The content of the short film must be related to the theme of Cultivating Play in Everyone.
Submit your entries online at our website.

Rules:
Video must be a maximum of five minutes.

The film should emphasize the importance of play for overall health.

The film should be appropriate for audiences of all ages.

She swung a leg over the seesaw and moved in search of something true and beautiful. She didn't know what exactly.

I'll know it when I see it.

Twigs crunched under her sneakers as she moved toward the still-standing bandstand where she had crawled as a toddler, maybe even learned to walk. Raising the camera, she captured a pink balloon floating past the trees toward the sun.

She followed the tree-lined footpath to the infamous duckpond. A pig-tailed girl broke pieces of bread off a loaf and threw them into the emerald water. Ducks flocked toward the bread, pecking. Two geese squawked and landed on the water. A bright-green leaf dangled on the stone wall.

Surrounded by nature, Olivia relaxed. She spotted her thinking bench tucked at the back of the pond beside a fountain and resumed the great debate.

On Olivia's thirty-second birthday, Gina was in New York for the annual fall gala. Olivia celebrated by making and eating half a tray of brownies. She sent Gina a picture. Olivia listened to the ticking clock, waiting for Gina to call or text back. Finally, toward the end of the night, a text came through: "HBD! We won second place in the regional competition. Heading out to celebrate. Hope you're enjoying the brownies."

That night, lying on the couch, the debate began with questions: *Is this the kind of relationship I really want? Should I stay with Gina, or is it time to end it?*

She pictured herself leaving the apartment, leaving Gina, and then rushing back. *Stay; it's safer.*

If, after the weekend, Olivia left the apartment, *their* apartment, would she be alone forever? Would the pain of cutting it off be worse than the loneliness?

To stay meant to trust that things could go back to how they were during the good times. The happy flutters, regular museum dates, laughs. Or to concede to the idea that relationships change, and the occasional date and laugh were enough.

Telling Gina the truth was better than stringing her along. Ending it might break Gina's heart. Ending it now, before kids and that sort of thing, was better than waiting.

Waiting might mean that she could fall back in love.

Two ducks lunged for the last piece of bread. As she leaned forward, recording, she pushed the questions away.

A sparrow dove from a tree and landed on a hot dog cart. By the time Olivia had the camera ready again, it had flown away. She slapped herself on the thigh. *Damn.* She might have called it Sparrow Vendor.

She stood and moved back down the path toward the playscape.

A family, at least what looked like a family, three kids all under four feet tall and two adults, set their backpacks down on a bench. Two of the kids ran full speed for the swings, the third for the slide. The one in the tee-ball uniform at the top of the slide said, "Watch this! Dad! Watch this! Watch this!" The boy kicked his legs and shouted, "Dad! Watch this!"

When the man picked his head up, the kid finally getting his attention, Olivia pressed record.

The pint-sized kid flew down the steep steel slide and landed in a pile of laughter on his back on the rubber pad. Mulch kicked up at the boy's feet—pure joy.

Olivia captured the whole glorious moment.

The kid sat up. His face, an explosion of giggles, turned into a frown. "Dad, did you see it, Dad? Dad?"

The man looked up from his phone for half a second, "I saw it, buddy. Go play."

The kid looked in Olivia's direction, and she gave him a smile and a thumb's up. She couldn't tell if he saw her or not, but when he was back at the top of the slide, he looked toward her, zoomed down again, and cracked himself up when he landed with another soft thud on his behind.

Olivia smiled at the kid's delight.

This will be an excellent shot for the film.

Camera in hand, she swung the bag over her shoulder and walked the other direction along the path, trees providing much-needed shade.

In the opening in the path just beyond the pond, a group of women wearing matching pink T-shirts set up for a charity walk. They opened boxes of bananas and lay them in neat rows. Balloons were tied to the corners of the table. Sometimes, with her camera, she became part of things, joined the activity. Other times, there might as well have been a brick wall between them, and she didn't know how to get around it.

Inclusion meant more than being together in the same place.

The balloons tied to their event tents called to her like those tied to a mailbox at a birthday party house, saying, "Come over here. The party is this way." She inched toward the table to get a better look. Maybe if she joined the walk, she could capture something meaningful, something profound.

A smiling woman with red hair and buckteeth motioned for Olivia to come forward. She held out a pen and said, "Just your name and date-a-birth is all we need." The smile didn't leave her face even when she talked. A ventriloquist's trick.

"What's the cost?" Olivia asked.

"Taking donations. Any amount," the woman said, still smiling.

Olivia didn't know the cause. "Remembering Stevie" was all she could read on the shirts.

"Do we get one of those shirts?" Olivia asked.

"Donate twenty or more to get a shirt," the woman said. She gazed across the crowd like she was looking out at a sea of fans and said, "It's gonna be a great day for walking. Seventy degrees, light breeze. Weather's perfect."

The line built up behind Olivia. She reached into the pocket of her jeans. She had a twenty and a five. She handed over the twenty and kept the five for coffee.

"What size would you like?" the woman asked.

She fell somewhere between small and medium, depending on the season. "Medium," she said. Just in case.

She stepped to the side and put on the shirt. At the starting area, a woman with a neon visor finished tying her shoe and stood up. She addressed the crowd, saying, "Thank you all for being here. Stevie was one of a kind. That cancer," she shook her head, "was a bitch."

Olivia's mind went to her brother. It always did when someone mentioned death. But she didn't want to be there thinking about death on a perfectly beautiful day.

When the loudspeaker boomed, announcing the start of the walk, Olivia stepped forward with the crowd. At the first corner, she peeled away from the group and perched herself on a rock on a slight hill. She angled the camera down on the walkers. Strangers made the perfect subjects for art because she could observe them without getting too close.

The battery light blinked red, and Olivia switched the dead one with the fresh one. She moseyed back toward the entrance. Some people sat on the ground writing in sidewalk chalk in the path near the fence. Olivia moved closer.

In large block letters, a group of teenagers wrote words on the concrete, decorated with swirls of yellow and blue and green. HOPE. PLAY. BELIEVE. LOVE.

A cuddly brown dog on a leash sniffed at her knee, and she scratched it on the head. She turned on the camera and pointed it toward the chalk words. When she got to the last one, the perfect word to end the short film, she zoomed in on the giant green letters:

LIVE.

CHAPTER 4

Olivia felt refreshed as she drove toward the community college, her weekly retreat into her passions—teaching and film.

Stopping at a salt marsh, she turned on the handheld camera and aimed it toward an osprey nest atop a pole near a coastal navigation marker. Calm ocean water tickled the shoreline. She waited for the osprey to leave the nest and dive down for supper. Maybe now, with her open schedule, she could come back in the mornings when she'd have better luck capturing this shot. Nature doesn't adhere to deadlines.

Finally, flapping wings rose out of the nest. A rise, spread wings, and a descent toward the water.

Swoosh. She moved the camera in sync with the bird. "I got you."

Alone in the film lab before any students or her co-leader arrived, Olivia spliced together the footage she'd taken. On the title page underneath "Imperturbable," she added a dedication to Mary Oliver and Werner Herzog. She held a loose fist against her chest, and a smile spread across her face. The hours it took to fit film into her life were worth it. Maybe there would be space for her to teach at the college full-time. Make her volunteer gig a paid gig.

There was a knock at the door. Standing at the entrance of the lab was Adrienne, a student in the club. "Have you seen my notebook? It's black and has my name on the inside cover."

Olivia looked around. "Sorry, Adrienne, I haven't seen it."

Adrienne shrugged her backpack off her shoulders and ruffled through it. Looking up at the screen, she asked, "What are you working on?"

Olivia tucked a strand of hair behind her ear and stretched her back. "My film project. I've been working on one too. Do you want to see it?"

Adrienne took a seat in the next chair, and Olivia pressed play for the first time on the five-minute short. A smile spread across Adrienne's face.

After watching, Adrienne said, "I can see why you named it that. This Rhode Island wildlife doesn't give a crap about us humans. This is really good."

"Thank you. Now let's get into the classroom, so we're not late."

They moved out of the lab and across the hall to the classroom where students had taken their seats. Tricia, the co-leader, directed everyone to the page in the book for the day's exploration.

As Tricia asked students to read a scene aloud from *Heart of Darkness*, Olivia reviewed her notes on Francis Ford Coppola's adaptation of the book in his film, *Apocalypse Now*. She'd read the book at least a dozen times and analyzed the film a handful. When they finished reading, Olivia stood next to the projector and spoke to the students.

"One of the major themes discussed for decades in this book and film is the darkness potentially inherent in all human hearts," Olivia said. "As you watch this scene, notice how Coppola plays with light and darkness. Is the theme evident to you here?"

She pressed play on the scene she had cued up.

At the end of the clip, she led the class in a discussion, starting by asking them what they noticed. She kept an eye on Tricia for signs of affirmation on her face. With Tricia's approval, maybe she would have a better chance of being hired by the college.

"I noticed the fog," one student said. "It seemed to add an element of confusion somewhere between darkness and light. Maybe there's a choice between good and evil, right and wrong."

"Interesting point. Anyone else?"

Olivia called on Adrienne.

"I thought John made a good point. I also wondered if Coppola wanted us to compare this to the scene on the bridge, where it was mostly dark except for the flares. It's making me think about how I might use light in my film project, since I'm exploring similar themes."

Olivia nodded. "Can you say a little more about that?"

"In my project, I'm looking at how people accept or reject support when they're going through challenging times. I hadn't thought about varying the lighting, but seeing how Coppola uses light to tell the story is exciting to me. Strategic use of fog is something I've never considered."

A couple of students chuckled.

"Very insightful," Olivia said. She thought about the statement.

Could there be right and wrong ways to get help?
She wasn't sure.

At the end of the discussion, Olivia asked for an update on projects and then sent the students out to work independently; she wanted a few extra minutes with Tricia to show her *Imperturbable*.

Olivia held her breath as Tricia studied the screen. Approval from Tricia meant approval from the college and approval from the world. Tricia's enthusiasm would tell Olivia that she was on the right track, someday ready to share her creation with an actual audience. And in the meantime, perhaps a job.

"Interesting take," Tricia said when it ended.

Olivia couldn't read her face. "I wanted to explore the beauty of nature compared to the dysfunction of man," she explained.

Tricia nodded.

"Do you like it?"

"Yeah, I like it. It's good."

Olivia yearned for more feedback. She debated asking another question, probing for affirmation, but Tricia packed her bag. Olivia stayed silent. The lukewarm response lingered in the air.

"I'll miss class next week for a doctor's appointment. You're good without me, yeah?"

"Of course," Olivia said. She took a deep breath and said, "Speaking of me flying solo in here, any chance I'd be able to throw my name in the ring for a full-time job?"

She felt her cheeks warming up, ready to go back to cool if Tricia said yes. She ran her fingers along the edge of the back of a chair.

Tricia shook her head. "Not unless you have an advanced degree," she said as she turned and walked out the door.

Her mom's voice shot like B-roll in her mind, *Do something that pays the bills. Art doesn't pay the bills.*

Olivia's head drooped in disappointment. She gathered her things and sat down at a student desk. She traced the grooves of the wooden desktop with a fingernail. She had spent the last ten years sitting at desks planning lessons and grading papers.

The faded yellow wood brought back so many memories. Exhaustion, especially just before and after the holidays when students were the most restless. Excitement from grading the paper of a ten-year-old who had finally mastered the difference between their, they're, and there. Frustration from being required to write robust comments for sixty fifth graders while ordering supplies for the science fair, fielding calls about a potential bullying situation, finishing the agenda for a department meeting, and preparing for the next lesson.

When June came around, all the best parts of teaching outweighed any challenges, and she enthusiastically signed up for another year. With the school closing, she didn't have the choice to go back this time.

She tapped her forehead.

Think, think, think.

There had been no call from anyone about a new school assignment. She couldn't teach at the college without an advanced degree. She briefly entertained the idea of packing everything into a van and driving out into the mountains. If only there were enough money for that.

She had one other idea.

One that made her stomach flip-flop and her heart speed up.

Uncle Tim and Aunt Margaret.

Her mother's pigheaded brother and his stoic wife.

She opened the social media app and clicked on Margaret's profile. She scrolled to the posts and read the first one:

Reminder, Friends!

In honor of my late husband Timothy "Tim" Roark, I'm pursuing two dreams this summer:

1) Leaving the role of assistant director behind and officially stepping into the director role. (Tim leaves big shoes to fill!)
2) Launching the Roark Fellowship for women in film. #closethegap

Thank you all who have been there for me these last few days. If you know any talented women (I know you do!) please let them know to apply to the fellowship as soon as possible.

xoxo Margaret

Olivia bit her lip. It was posted only a few hours ago. *What happened to Tim?*

She remembered birthday cards signed, "xoxo Margaret & Tim." The x's and o's an insufficient stand-in for real love. At least her mom was open about how she felt.

Olivia believed her when she had said, "I'll never go to one of these again," after Billy's funeral.

She reread the post. A fellowship for women in film. *That could be me.*

She opened her phone and checked to see if she still had Margaret's number. She didn't.

If she texted her mom for Margaret's number, she would open herself up to other conversations that she didn't want to have.

She opened Margaret's profile and searched for her number. Her hand trembled slightly at the thought of speaking to her aunt, who was practically a stranger. What if she didn't know what to say?

Finding the number, she opened a text message and wrote: "Margaret. It's Olivia. I'm so sorry for your loss. Please let me know if there's anything you need."

Bubbles appeared immediately; Margaret was responding.

Olivia held her breath.

She read the response. "Thank you. Funeral tomorrow in Boston. Your mother can't make it. Please come. Christ Church at 11:00 a.m."

She stood from the desk and swung her backpack over her shoulder. It made sense to her that her mom wouldn't attend. But should she? Just because Margaret hadn't been around much when she was a kid didn't mean Olivia couldn't be there for Margaret.

She texted, "I'll be there."

What would it be like to see Margaret again?

CHAPTER 5

Olivia rubbed her temples. *Where do I go from here?*

On Saturday night, in the stillness of the bedroom, she breathed in the final quiet moments. Gina would be home by the end of the night. She stared at the ceiling, willing the stress to melt out of her body. Her mind kept going back to the conversation in the cafeteria from the day before—two suited men standing before a group of teachers delivering the news. Ten years of work washed away like a coastal community in a hurricane. The local news cycle might pick it up for a minute, but in a few weeks, people would barely remember it happened.

Olivia rolled over and faced Gina's side of the bed. *Would the same thing happen to us? How did this all go wrong?*

A memory flickered to life.

A week after turning nineteen, Olivia marched into a museum holding a student pass. She had taken a run that morning, something she only did on the mornings when she couldn't sleep and stopped for breakfast on the way back to the college dorms. She showered quickly and dressed in her favorite fall color, maroon.

In the museum, Olivia searched for the VIP tour guide she had hired through the museum website to give her a private tour. She stood under the "Tours" sign on one wall of the large square room and looked up. In the sparkling white light of the museum, each tier became its own palace. The clear glass banister around each level allowed a glimpse of people reading exhibit signs and darting in and out of rooms; so many floors, so much potential.

Olivia pulled up the sleeve of her sweater and checked the time on her Timex sports watch. *Early.*

Bouncing on her toes, she read the list of exhibits. Stories of Cinema. Films of the '80s. Foreign Film Debuts in the United States. A type of freedom came with going into a place like that. In the classroom, she was limited to the pages of books and film clips selected by professors. At the museum, she was free.

She would explore without a hired guide in all the subsequent visits, but to begin, having someone to lead her through the amazing maze of history and culture would help her get her bearings. Sometimes having a map made the journey a little more efficient.

A man in a suit jacket linked by the arm to a woman who smelled like her own private garden scanned their tickets and went through the turnstiles. A moment later, a slender, smiling woman with bouncing brown hair danced toward her. A rose-colored scarf hung loosely around her chest. She introduced herself as Gina Wings, part-time tour guide, part-time student, full-time art and life enthusiast. To Olivia, Gina was everything.

Together they walked from room to room like two eclectic librarians. Olivia's scattered eagerness was balanced by Gina's calm intelligence. Since then, they had spent most of their days together until a year ago, when Gina took the job as communications director, and things shifted.

Olivia's body ached as she stepped from the bed. The cold floor creaked under her feet. In the kitchen, she turned on the light above the stove. She opened the cupboard for a tea bag and pulled the weightless cardboard container from the shelf. *Empty.* Olivia rolled her eyes in the low light of the kitchen. *Fucking Gina.*

The first argument happened over the same annoying habit.

A few weeks into her new job, Gina left for her first work trip. Being the director of a network of museums required frequent travel. The following day, Olivia went to the cupboard to make coffee and found that the jar of beans was gone. Olivia messaged Gina.

Gina responded, "Wasn't sure what the coffee sitch at the hotel would be like."

That alone might have been fine. Olivia picked up coffee from the store and continued her day. On the night that Olivia expected Gina to come home, Gina messaged, "Be home by five."

Olivia prepared Gina's favorite meal, honey garlic salmon and rosemary roasted potatoes. At five o'clock, she set dinner on the table, but Gina wasn't home. The minutes passed, and then the hours. Six, seven, eight, nine.

When Gina walked in the door at ten, Olivia shoved a Tupperware container at her. "Please don't take all the coffee again." She could feel the coolness of the words as they came out of her mouth.

Gina apologized, saying, "Some people wanted to stop for drinks and a poker game. Couldn't say no."

"You could have given me a head's up," Olivia responded.

"You're right. I will next time," Gina said.

Sometimes she did, sometimes she didn't. Olivia grew accustomed to scraping Gina's dinners into plastic containers, stacking them so high in the fridge that they nearly toppled over. Over time, Olivia stopped cooking for two and acclimated to the solitude of Gina's work trips. Sometimes she worked on film projects or watched movies with Brad, her neighbor, in the apartment upstairs.

But she ached for the comfort Gina used to give. Lately, the bed was cold and empty, even when Gina was home. The traveling hadn't caused the distance, but it didn't help either. Their connection, once held together with long conversations, intimate sex, and inside jokes, had faded away like morning fog, dissipating slowly. Barely noticeable until it's completely gone.

With the tea bags likely folded in the corner of Gina's suitcase, Olivia left the kitchen and went back to bed.

She stared at a watermark in the ceiling and tried to rest.

"Olivia?"

The door opened.

She couldn't end it tonight. There were too many things left to figure out. Where would she go? She had nowhere. Her mom lived in some city out west in one of those states Olivia couldn't place on a map. Idaho? Montana? Colorado? Whichever it was, Olivia wouldn't go anyway; they hadn't talked in years. Plus, there was the whole job disaster.

Olivia turned in the covers and stared at the light blue wall. Since meeting Gina, she hadn't put a lot of energy into other relationships. She'd catch herself with her phone in her palm, ready to call an old friend, only to put it down again a moment later. Aside from Brad, with whom she watched movies once a month, she didn't see anyone regularly. She wished she had known that friendships would die if they weren't nurtured. "How to Adult" should be a class taught in school.

I'm going to be completely alone.

Olivia turned toward Gina. "Did you take the tea with you?"

"Why does it matter? You could buy more," Gina said in a condescending tone.

"That's not the point," Olivia said and rolled back to face the window.

Olivia's body stiffened in the bed. The air in the room, laced with tension, threatened to suffocate her.

Suitcase wheels scuffed against the hardwood floors. Gina dumped clothes in and around the laundry basket as she did at the end of every trip. She set her phone on the nightstand with a thud and retreated down the hallway toward the bathroom. A moment later, the sound of the shower came from the next room.

Olivia examined Gina's mess. Clothes littered the room. On the bedside table, Gina's phone blinked ominously.

Who is texting her at this time of night?

Olivia moved to Gina's side of the bed. Her hand shook as she pulled Gina's phone off the table. She clicked the button on the side. A preview of a message appeared on the screen. Someone named Doctor Martin had written, "Let's hang out when you get back," followed by a purple devil emoji. The message sent a shooting pain through her body.

No one's doctor sends emojis like that one through text. Who is this person?

One more reason why ending the relationship was the best next step. Why did it feel like separating bone from sinew?

Fucking Gina.

Olivia turned to the watercolor paintings of cardinals that hung on the wall next to the window. "How did we get here?" she asked the cardinals.

Somewhere in between *I don't deserve this* and *How am I supposed to move on?* her thoughts turned on her, saying, *Maybe if you hadn't been working so much, you'd still be in love. You should have kept the romance alive. You should have seen this coming. You didn't do enough.*

Olivia wiped her face with her sleeve and replaced the phone where she'd found it. She tucked herself under the covers and lay still in the darkness. Tears soaked her pillow, and she told herself to breathe.

Stop. It's going to be okay.

Olivia shrank into the pillow. She felt small and weak and worthless.

I'm already alone.

The door to the bedroom opened, and the mattress rose beneath Olivia as Gina slid beneath the covers on her side of the bed. Olivia opened her eyes and looked out the window. Stars glimmered pompously in the night sky.

The moon was full, and Olivia's heart was empty.

She pretended to sleep.

CHAPTER 6

Light streamed through the stained glass in shades of red and blue, illuminating the image of St. Francis surrounded by birds.

Olivia stood at the back of the church with her hands in the pockets of her black dress pants. Nervousness fluttered down her arms. She shifted her weight to make space between the waistline and her hips. The stitching formed shallow lines in her skin. She kept meaning to buy a new pair but hadn't gotten around to it. Incense drifted in wisps of woody smoke from a small metal bowl suspended by a chain in the priest's hands.

She opened her phone, scrolled past a message from Gina, and found the text from Margaret. She reread the words: "Thank you. Funeral tomorrow in Boston. Your mother can't make it. Please come. Christ Church at 11:00 a.m."

Anticipation built within her. Would this be a chance to form a connection with Aunt Margaret?

A pungent flare of women's perfume accompanied by clacking shoes announced Margaret's arrival. Olivia spun around.

Margaret stepped through the ornate wooden doors. White hair, stark against the black blazer, hung down to her shoulders.

Olivia stepped toward her.

Be cool.

"Hello, Olivia. Thank you for coming," Margaret said, her tone formal and her voice calm. She pursed her thin, pink lips. "Let's go find a seat."

Margaret moved toward the front of the church as if she were wearing stilts, legs long and stiff. There was a tightness about her from the stick-straight arms of her blazer down to her perfectly tailored slacks.

Olivia gazed toward the altar, surveying the empty church. They still had thirty minutes until the service began. Olivia groaned inwardly at the awkward silence. *Where do I even start?*

"I'm so sorry for your loss," Olivia said as they entered the first pew.

Margaret took off her blazer and folded it neatly on the bench. The pressed white shirt hung loosely on her slight frame. *Get this woman a cheeseburger.*

Fumbling for what to do or say, Olivia took a tissue from her pocket and blew her nose. She balled it up and shoved it back into her pocket. The priest straightened the Bible on the pulpit. None of the words that came to Olivia's mind felt right. *"How are you doing?" Insensitive. "I'm sorry." Redundant. "What's new with you?" Asinine.* Still, a strong urge pulled at her to fill the silence.

"It's been a while," Olivia said. Her arms twitched, wanting to reach out and hug Margaret, wanting it to feel familiar. Instead, she held her elbows.

Margaret nodded.

Olivia didn't know what to make of it. Margaret had asked her to be there, yet she felt so far away. Disappointment rose within her. *Why did I come here?*

After several minutes, Margaret spoke. "While we still have some time, I'd love to talk to you about the film fellowship."

Olivia's eyes widened. *Uncle Tim* is lying dead five feet away, and this is what she wants to talk about?

Despite her incredulity, Olivia nodded. If this was what Margaret wanted to talk about in the hour of her husband's funeral, she would oblige.

"Sure," she said.

"Have you given it any thought? I know you must've seen it in my post. More women like you in the industry would be a good thing."

Olivia didn't know what to say. It would be exciting to have a second chance to work in film. At the same time, insecurities lit inside her like the candles around the casket. "I don't know. I've just been teaching. I've only done a few projects."

Olivia thought of the short film she had just made and her student's smile in response to it. There were so many stories not yet told.

Margaret nodded. "You'd be working with other mentors and me on the set of our TV show, *Murder in Morristown*. It would be an opportunity for you to pursue a real career."

A real career?

Her words stung. Olivia swallowed. "I'll think about it."

Margaret jumped up from the seat. "I told them no lilies." She marched toward the pots of flowers. She picked the lilies out one by one and walked them to the trash.

Olivia considered the opportunity presented by Margaret. Pros: Getting back into film and back on track to her childhood dream of being a film director. Moving to a new place far away from Gina. Adventure. Cons: Getting help from a distant family member. Starting over in her career back at the base of a mountain while everyone else was nearing the top.

After the funeral, Olivia, head spinning, took the elevator past the apartment she shared with Gina and went straight to Brad's. A few months back, she had put a sign in the lobby: Monthly Film Club! Below the title, she listed her contact information, and the first club meeting happened in her and Gina's apartment.

As schedules got busy and people moved, a group of six whittled down to two, Olivia and Brad, a young accountant with a love for movies.

Olivia let herself into the meticulous apartment where Brad had lived for at least the last five years. He talked from time to time about buying a house, saying things like, "Well, I do have enough for a down payment," but from what Olivia could tell, he had no real intention of moving.

The place smelled like salt and cheese. Her mouth watered as he pulled two plain white plates out of the cupboard.

"What do you want to watch tonight?" he asked, handing her a plastic cup of iced tea.

Olivia took a seat in her corner of the leather couch. "Do you mind if we talk for a few minutes first? I want to run something by you." She had prepared what she would say on the way over. Brad's opinion as a fellow TV and movie enthusiast, and, if Olivia was being honest, one of her only real friends, mattered to her.

"Shoot," he said. He scooped a handful of nachos from the dish in the center of the table onto a plate.

She shared the details of the school closing and let out a sigh, "So I need to figure out what's next."

"How are you holding up?" he asked.

"I'm okay," she said.

He nodded. "Schools are literally everywhere. You'll find another spot."

Olivia scratched her head. He wasn't wrong. "Thanks for saying that. I'm not sure what I'll do next."

"Would you really leave teaching?"

The taste of bitter olive filled her mouth.

I'm not leaving anyone.

Yet even considering something outside of teaching activated the guilt trigger.

"There's a lot to think about for sure," she said. Condensation dripped down the side of the plastic cup. She knew that this might be an opportunity to do something different, to change her plans. Still, she didn't want to admit that she didn't want to go back to teaching. It would be a sin, a crime against teachers, to change course now. She was a teacher. That was who she was.

But a small voice inside her whispered, *This might be the chance to go for the dream. To tell the stories that haven't been told. To spend all day creating and moving and bringing something to life that hasn't existed before.*

She swallowed the tea. A final ice cube, thin as a wood chip, clung to the inner rim at the bottom of the cup. Her hands were cold. She hadn't planned for this change; it was thrust on her like an unwanted hug. And now that she was here, she didn't know what to do. It seemed like a sign from the universe that it was time for a change, but what if it didn't work out?

Brad shoved a chip slathered in chicken, cheese, and jalapeños into his mouth.

"I'm not sure I want to go back. There's this film fellowship for women that I'm thinking about applying to." She held her breath and looked at the ground. "I've been teaching for a decade, and I like it and everything, but… I'm not sure what to do." She groaned slightly. "The fellowship would be an opportunity to work on a real TV show with the professionals. I'd get to learn how they do it in the field instead of just reading about it. What do you think?"

"I mean, you could," he said noncommittally.

Anxiety chewed on Olivia's rib cage. "What are you thinking?"

Brad sighed. "It seems like a lot, figuring out how to start over in a totally new career. I don't think I could do it after putting in so much time. Plus, say you get the fellowship, where would you live? Who would you go with? Wouldn't you be lonely? And, film industry, you have to make something amazing for it to pay off. That could take years."

She shifted in her corner of the couch, propping herself up onto her elbow like she was at an interview. She mulled over his questions, each one of them valid.

He wiped his face with a cloth napkin.

All the movies she had seen ran through her mind like a kineograph. "You're right. It could take years. I still think I want to try. I think I could make something unique."

He coughed.

Her heart raced, eager for approval.

Tell me it's okay to pursue this.

He gulped iced tea and then said, "What will you do if you don't get in?"

His questions hit the tips of her nerves, and she squirmed on the couch.

She switched tactics like she was trying to convince him the woman she liked wasn't a bad idea after talking for hours about all the red flags. "They give us mentors. A stipend. Housing! We get to work on a real show with real actors. My name might be in the credits. I might not be able to make a blockbuster film yet, but I know I can make something interesting with my take on nature versus nurture. There's more to be done there."

"Yeah, you have some convincing ideas in that department. That's true," he said, licking his fingers. "Still, think about the likelihood of succeeding in a new career in a new industry at thirty-something, especially one of these legacy, people-you-know type industries like film… You'll probably spend a decade changing batteries before you see any real action."

The leather couch clung to her leg. She resisted the urge to tell Brad about Margaret. If she succeeded, she wanted it to come from her own merit and hard work, not from a family connection. She wasn't sure if Margaret would want to help her either way. "If I don't submit an application, I'll never know."

"Good point," he said. Then he added, as if he could sense the strength of her desire, "I'm not trying to be a downer here. I'm looking out for you. You know I'll support you either way."

"I know," she said, reaching for a plate. "Are you ready to choose a movie?"

He nodded and clicked on the TV.

She stared at the screen, but her mind wandered.

At the end of the movie, Olivia watched the credits roll like she always did. Kevin. Richard. James. Donna. Tony. Barry. Walter.

She looked away in quiet disgust.

"Gina coming home soon?" he asked when Olivia stood, reminding her she wanted to ask him about the possibility of renting his second bedroom, eventually.

"She came home last night."

"What does she think about the fellowship?"

"It doesn't matter what she thinks," she said, more sharply than she intended. "I need to make the decision on my own."

"So, you'd leave her for this?" Brad stopped shaking the cup of ice in his hand.

"I think I'm going to leave her either way."

"You think?" His eyes opened wide, disbelieving.

Olivia started to understand why Brad had lived in the same city where he grew up working at the bank around the corner living in the same apartment he had lived in since he graduated college around the same time she did. Some people don't cope well with change. Even the thought of it can toss them into a full-blown identity crisis.

I'm in one now.

"It's not just the annoyance, Brad. I saw texts on her phone from another person." Fresh anger bubbled in Olivia's chest.

Fucking Gina.

Brad put the cup down and crossed his arms. "What? How?"

"She left the phone beside me when she got home, and I saw some messages that made it clear she's cheating on me. Part of me thinks she did it on purpose."

"Why didn't you tell me that before?"

Olivia fidgeted with a torn piece of napkin. "It's embarrassing."

"You've read the messages?"

"Only a couple of them." Olivia's chest tightened at the thought of the last one she'd read. *"I'm saving your number in my phone as Doctor ;) so Olivia doesn't have a clue."*

"Shit, dude, I'm sorry."

"It's all good. It won't last. Once a cheater, always a cheater. When this chick finds out what she's like, it will be over for them too."

Wouldn't it?

A feeling of toxic sludge crept up from deep inside her intestines, and she slapped it back down.

CHAPTER 7

Later that night, heavy evening rain slashed against the window; a halo of mist formed around a single streetlight. Olivia stuffed the gray towel into the crevice of the window to prevent water from dripping onto the tattered couch and turned on the lamp. She folded herself into a pretzel on the couch, opened a novel, and stared at the bookmarked page.

Gina puttered around the apartment, opening and shutting cabinets, watering plants in the shower, and seeming, to Olivia, to be practicing which tactics would get a reaction out of her (soon to be ex) girlfriend.

The only reaction Olivia gave that night was a silent eye roll. Annoyance had stitched a translucent patch over Olivia's eyes, forming a permanent filter through which she saw Gina. Her love for Gina had been windblown, a green leaf in a pile of brown, so impossible to find that no one bothered to look.

Olivia put the book down and pulled her laptop open to peruse the fellowship website. She tapped the word "fellowship," and a web browser opened from the hyperlink. "The Roark Fellowship" appeared in bold navy letters across the top.

Olivia scrolled through the page and stopped at the description:

> *Women are creative and talented, but they make up a small percentage of directors, cinematographers, writers, and crew members. The Roark Fellowship aims to address this gap by providing easy access to training and jobs for women in film.*

The mission to close the gender representation gap in the film industry resonated with her. Programs like this one, addressing inequality, promised access to experience, training, and a network in exchange for time and work. She browsed through the content of the fellowship. She'd get to work on the set of the newly popular show, *Murder in Morristown*.

She scrolled down to the application directions. "Submit a résumé and cover letter. Respond to the application question. Share a link to one short project." The application criteria were outlined like a recipe. Do these things and, voilà, you'll arrive. Except, in this case, according to the webpage, there was a panel of judges on the other end ready to evaluate her skills.

Then she looked at the deadline.

June 30.

Today.

Olivia shot up from the couch. She put on the kettle to make instant coffee, a jolt of caffeine, and went back to her computer. She clicked the bold "Apply Now" button and read the first question: "Tell us, in five hundred words or less, why you want to be a Roark Fellow."

"What do you want to be when you grow up?" An innocent question asked by every adult—at holiday parties, on the first day of school. She would stand, corners of her lips drawing downward, waiting for them to talk about the stuff that really mattered like how she felt or what she thought about growing up with so many worries.

Every time people asked what she wanted to *be*, she answered, standing up a smidge straighter each time. "Cinnamon-tographer." "Cinematographer." "Film director." Until everyone knew she wanted to do something with film, and so they stopped asking that question and moved to the next logical thing—marriage. Questions became, "Got a man in your life? Any prospects?"

To these she had formed the generic response, "You'll be the first to know," said with a wry smile.

If only she had known what to say to get the advice she most needed, maybe she would have figured out a few things sooner. Maybe social dynamics and relationships would have been easier to navigate, to understand.

Since middle school, everything was confusing.

At the seventh-grade dance, Olivia stood against the wall with her arms crossed like all the other kids. Whispers passed from one kid to the next, "Michelle likes Matt. Pass it on." An upbeat song played and an outgoing girl with butterfly clips in her hair dragged a couple friends onto the gym floor. Olivia tapped a foot to the beat.

"You like this song?" Maddie asked in a curious, judgment-free voice. Maddie, like Olivia, wore high-top sneakers and jeans. Maddie donned a basketball jersey; Olivia, a vintage hockey sweatshirt. Most of their classmates wore jeans and crop tops or spaghetti strapped tank tops. Wisps of fabric.

"I guess," Olivia said. The beat went up and down like the dribble of a basketball, and Olivia's leg bounced with it. She wouldn't be caught dead dancing, but she let her foot go up and down, just a little, in the dark corner of the gym.

The girl with the butterfly clips skipped over. She was dressed like a snowflake, head-to-toe in white: white halter top, white cargo pants, white Adidas sneakers with gold stripes. Her arms flailed up and down like she was a ballerina in a performance of *The Nutcracker*. "Liv, Maddie, hurry up, come with me. Michelle and Matt are going to kiss," she shrieked with excitement.

Olivia let herself be dragged from the gym and down the hallway past the lockers. School felt different on a Friday night—their playground. When they got to the girls' locker room, she hung back with Maddie. A few other classmates gathered in a circle around Michelle, who sat on the bench in front of a row of lockers where Olivia had changed for practice a few hours before.

"Are you going to do it?" one of the girls asked.

Michelle nodded vigorously. The door swung open. Matt flew into the room, shoved from behind by some of the guys.

"There's too many people here," Matt pleaded in a high-pitched voice. "You brought the lesbians in here too?" His voice was cartoonish, but the words were prickly and sharp. Olivia had never described herself in that way before. Never talked about her crushes or budding romantic feelings.

"Just do it real quick," one of the guys said. "You're a chicken." The focus stayed on Matt and Michelle despite Matt's attempt at a diversion. Olivia was grateful for that.

Matt looked side to side, lunged forward, pecked Michelle on the lips and darted back out the door. The guys behind him hooted and hollered until the sounds faded.

"That was lame," one of the girls said.

Then all eyes turned toward Olivia and Maddie.

"You two should kiss," butterfly clips said.

Olivia and Maddie looked at each other and started laughing.

"Ew," Olivia said. "We're just friends."

"Yeah, gross," Maddie said.

Olivia didn't admit that she would have said yes. She didn't admit that she would have kissed Maddie in the corner of the locker room or anywhere else until years later. And only to herself. There was no one to talk to about those feelings; no one ever asked, and it never came up. No one else she knew was like her. Until college. Until Gina.

Fucking Gina.

Olivia clicked back to the main screen to review the details of the fellowship again as an answer started composing itself in her mind. Words popped out on the page. Women. Film. Opportunity. Stipend. Network.

Something stirred inside her, warming like wax in a burning candle.

The floor creaked. "What are you doing?" Gina asked casually.

"Nothing," Olivia answered calmly, closing the laptop. "Just looking at stuff online." Olivia forced a smile.

"I'm going to go up to bed. Are you coming?" Gina asked.

This had become their nightly routine when Gina was home, and they each played their part.

"I'm going to stay down here tonight," Olivia said. "I tweaked my back running this morning, and it's better for me to sleep on the couch." She adjusted the heating pad against her shoulders and switched it on.

"Are you sure?" Gina asked, pulling a sweatshirt over her head.

"I need to be propped up tonight. I won't get any sleep otherwise."

Gina nodded.

Olivia knew a desire for harmony would obstruct either of them from saying more.

The stairs groaned under Gina's slippered feet.

Olivia opened the laptop. In the small white box, Olivia typed her response. "Working in film has been a dream of mine since I was a kid. As a film major in college, I learned technique, and I applied that knowledge to create short films. I want to be a Roark Fellow to pursue a dream. I believe I would be an asset to your team because I'm passionate."

She read what she had written and deleted it, starting again. *This is a once-in-a-lifetime opportunity.*

The words felt stale when she read them back, so she erased them. *How can I tell them my "why" in fewer than five hundred words?*

She typed again, "How many female directors do you know? How many of them make films juxtaposing nature with our largely artificial lives?"

She listened to the rain pinging on the window. A bang of thunder reverberated off the walls. She kept typing and retyping until she was partially satisfied. At least she'd written the truth.

The storm slackened to a light drizzle. Olivia attached a link to the file of her short film to the last question of the application. The cursor hovered over the "submit" button. She went back to the top and read the application again, changing some words.

A few minutes before midnight, she clicked "submit" and let go of the breath she'd been holding. She laid back on the couch pillow and let the *drip, drip, drip* lull her to sleep, a soft smile hovering on her lips.

CHAPTER 8

Today's the day I have to end this.

Olivia, sore and stiff and sad, rose from the couch and went to the kitchen. She put on a pot of coffee and turned on the TV. On the screen, a bright-orange gecko, tailless, looked directly at the camera from its place on a rock. The shot cut to a woman wearing horn-rimmed glasses and a lab coat who said, "When a gecko feels threatened, it can self-mutate, detaching its tail from its body."

Really?

"Scientists call this process 'autotomy.' The tail, split from the body, continues to move for several minutes after being cut clean. The gecko, free from danger, moves to safety while the predator is left confused."

The tailless gecko reappeared, moving across a rock. Olivia tilted her head, surveying the odd, stumpy creature. The will to escape danger is a powerful force.

When the coffee stopped dripping, she poured a steaming cup. On the couch, she curled up under a fleece blanket and savored the stillness of morning. A stream of sunlight crawled through the window by the two potted plants. "Maybe I should water you guys," she said to the plants. "You're looking a little dry and droopy."

The brown leaves sagged over the edge of the terracotta pots.

Probably too late.

From the bedroom came the *thud* of Gina's feet on the floor. On the outside, Olivia was a duck, still and calm. She held the red New Hampshire moose mug, a relic from one of their first weekend getaways, steady between her palms. Inside, however, a war began. There were groans, fits of protest, and preparations for battle.

Gina emerged from the bedroom, poured herself a mug of coffee, and joined Olivia on the couch.

Breathe. You can do this.

"How'd you sleep?" Gina asked.

"Pretty well," Olivia said. "How about you?"

"Great. It's so good to sleep in my own bed again."

Olivia squeezed the mug and took another sip, tipping the cup all the way back. *Empty. Damn.*

She stood and refilled the mug.

How come I can rehearse things hundreds of times and still not feel prepared when the moment comes?

She shuffled back to her spot on the couch, swallowed, and blurted, "I think we need to talk."

"What's up?" Gina asked. Her eyes moved rapidly, and her face drained of color.

"This is really uncomfortable," Olivia started, "but I've been thinking…"

Spit it out.

"I think we should break up."

As soon as she said those first few words, Gina began to cry. Gina cried at everything.

Olivia held still. She gave Gina the easy way out by not bringing up the texts. If she brought them up, Gina would immediately be on the defensive, spitting out excuses, lies, justifications, or, worse, truths. Gina had left the relationship long ago. Maybe Olivia had too.

"Why?" Gina asked. She wiped the tears away and straightened her face.

Olivia swallowed and said, "Things haven't been good for a while now."

Gina crossed her arms and looked sternly down at Olivia as if the tears a moment before had been an act. "You never want to hang out with my friends or me," she accused.

Olivia folded her arms. "Your friends are a bunch of animals. All you do is drink and pass money back and forth."

"At least we do *something*. All you do is work and run around with that camera attached to your wrist like some kind of paparazzi freak."

All the air left Olivia, and she gasped. She wanted the conversation to end. Silence hung between them. Pain rose in Olivia's throat from the deepest part of her gut. The image of the stumpy gecko squirmed in her mind.

Maybe humans survive through autotomy too.

"The last ten years together, and this is how you want to leave things?" Olivia asked.

"Don't pin this all on me," Gina said, stomping down the hall.

"Where are you going?" Olivia asked. She didn't want to know the answer.

Gina yelled back from halfway down the hall, "I'm going to stay with a friend for a while, give you some time to figure your shit out."

Olivia wiped her face with the sleeves of her sweatshirt. *Why does doing the right thing sometimes feel so wrong?*

Later, when Olivia stepped into the shower, the tears came. First in slow drips and then in sobs. She could call Gina, apologize, plead for things to go back to normal. *We can start again. You can be the Gina you were before that job. We can be the us before the arguments.* But, for so many reasons, they couldn't go back.

She sobbed and breathed. Breathed and sobbed. Water poured down her face and back. *It's going to be okay. You're going to be okay*, she repeated, like a mantra she might someday believe.

She stepped out of the shower and wrapped herself in a soft towel. She walked to the bedroom, feet pressed against the cold floor, and laid down on the bed.

Tears careened uncontrollably down her cheeks. Every part of her body ached.

I got what I wanted. I should feel better than this.

The weight of loneliness pressed into her chest.

It's going to be okay.

She didn't know if she believed it.

Five days passed. With each day, time spent crying decreased and more space opened to plan for the future.

On her fifth day as a single, unemployed woman, Olivia browsed the shelves of the supermarket looking for Frosted Flakes, her favorite comfort food.

She reached for the cereal and tucked it into the basket. As she moved toward the milk, her phone chimed.

Gina?

For a brief second, nervousness flickered inside her. She hadn't heard from Gina, and she wasn't sure she wanted to.

She looked down at the phone.

Unknown number.

She opened the message.

The text said, "Hi Olivia. This is JD, Margaret Roark's assistant. I hope you had a chance to read the email. Congratulations! However, we have a situation we need to discuss. Please call me when you have a moment."

In line at the register, she opened the email on her phone. "Congratulations, you've been accepted to the Roark Fellowship. We were impressed with your application and would love to offer you a spot. Please read the attached information and complete the survey letting us know your decision."

Olivia yelped with excitement. A grin broke across her face.

Wow, wow, wow. I got in.

"Excuse me, ma'am, the line is moving," a man huffed from behind her.

She stepped forward without looking up from her phone. She controlled her shoulders as they tried to start their own dance party. A shoulder party. *Ya, ya, ya, ya, ya.*

Olivia flipped through names in her contact list. *Who can I call?*

The man behind her grunted.

She turned around and grinned at him. "I got into a really cool program. Just found out."

"Good for you, lady. Now let's move it," he said. He reeked of cigarette smoke and bad luck. The kind of guy who bought a lotto ticket twice a day and never won.

He scratched at his temples and shifted the basket in his hand.

She shuffled forward and put the half gallon of sweating milk onto the conveyor belt. As the checker scanned the groceries, Olivia reread the email, *Congratulations.*

It was real; she hadn't been imagining it.

Outside in the parking lot, she dialed JD's number.

"Hi, JD, this is Olivia Gabriel."

"Olivia! Thank you for calling me back. I have good news and bad news. Good news: Congratulations! You've been accepted as a Roark Fellow. I definitely want you to celebrate this moment." She paused.

"That's amazing! Thank you so much," Olivia said, mentally packing her bags.

"Now for the not-so-great news. When we were making the assignments, we couldn't place you as a mentee to the assistant director, so we slotted you in to be the location manager. We know that wasn't what you wanted, but your aunt said you might have some experience planning events and logistics for the students in your classroom, so we're hoping you'll be excited about this. And you'll still be able to learn a lot, of course. We make sure each fellow gets a rotation as first assistant director if they want one. Are you in?"

Olivia wiped beads of sweat from her forehead. She felt slightly annoyed at Margaret for assuming. At the same time, she wasn't wrong. Olivia's experiences as a teacher prepared her to handle this type of thing.

Either way, an undeniable excitement washed over her. "I'm in," she said. "I'm really looking forward to it."

"If you have any questions after reviewing the details, feel free to reach out. We're looking forward to seeing you next week. We'll book the flight and send you a confirmation. The rest of the information is in the email."

Olivia thanked her. She opened the email and reviewed the instructions. The show would be filmed at Jasper Equestrian, a sprawling family horse ranch on the outskirts of a small town. A nice place to live and a thousand miles away.

She scrolled down and continued reading. For participating in the fellowship, fellows would receive a housing stipend along with a modest salary for working on the show. There were pictures of women in various positions on a set and beneath the photo were the words, "The film industry, though male-dominated, thrives when women are involved."

Olivia smiled.

This is the best next step.

She picked up her phone. Her fingers hovered over the contact list as she went through her mental file of people-to-call-at-proud-moments.

She called Brad, and his phone went to voicemail. She left a brief message: "Hey Brad, I hope you're having a good day. Wanted to tell you that I got into the fellowship. Give me a call back if you have time. Otherwise, we'll catch up soon."

She had no one else to tell. How was that possible?

I really need to make some friends.

She stroked the miniature stuffed sloth that hung from the rearview mirror and started cheering, "We got in." Clap. "We got in." Clap.

Goosebumps prickled on her arms.

She addressed her companion, "What do you think little dude? You excited?" The car rumbled backward and then forward. The sound of the dying engine grated at her ears. "What will we do with this car? How will we pay our bills? This stipend isn't big. They give us housing, though, and food. That's huge."

Sloth bounced around in the summer light.

"What's that? You think we'll make it work like we always do?" She pulled the steering wheel and navigated through the maze of cars and pedestrians. "And if this works, my man, we'll be set. Life will be good." She turned onto the highway and aimed toward home. Road work was a constant, which meant permanent delays. She turned on her favorite Lizzo song and sang all the way home.

Back in the apartment, she poured milk into a bowl and added a handful of Frosted Flakes a few bites at a time so they wouldn't get soggy.

"Cheers to our new adventure," she said to the tiger on the box.

She spent the rest of the night packing and thinking about whether or not she should say something to Principal Maylor or any of the other teachers. Part of her didn't want to say goodbye. She knew once she said those words, that would be it. She would mean it. Not only words, but also a promise. She understood now why sometimes people left without saying goodbye.

The allure of a new beginning pulled her forward. She fingered the ridge of the zipper on the suitcase. She would fly to a place she had never been to follow a dream delayed. *You're really doing it,* she thought, a surge of nervousness passing through her.

She texted Gina, "Hey G. I'm going to move out this weekend. I'll pay you through the end of the month."

Gina responded, "K."

Olivia clicked the phone, and the screen went blank. She called around and made arrangements to sell her car to a lot and store her few totes of possessions in a five-by-ten storage unit.

After the final box was shut, she changed into sweatpants and sunk into the couch. On the TV, the scientist held an iguana. "As they grow, iguanas shed their skin. If you see them rubbing their backs against objects in their cage, they might be working to shed a patch of skin."

Olivia grimaced, heart thumping, feeling as if she was shedding a skin of her own.

Am I doing the right thing?

CHAPTER 9

Olivia pressed her forehead to the window at the back of the small aircraft and swallowed a wave of nausea from the most recent bout of turbulence on the second flight of the day. There was nothing direct about getting to Jasper Cliffs on what the flight attendant announced just might be the hottest day on record.

She looked down at the printed map spread across her lap, a simple grid of streets. At least the town itself would be easy to navigate.

She flipped the map over to the blank side. A clean slate. At the top of the page, she wrote, "Career Plan." She had written thousands of plans as a teacher and, though not all of them went as she thought they would go, she was better off with one than without one.

On the page, she wrote, "One: Understand the path from fellowship to full-time." If this was going to work, she needed income. The plane bounced, and her stomach spun.

Breathe. You have enough to get you through right now. She had done the calculations and knew she would be okay, but still, the thought of running out of money sent her into a hot ball of anxiety.

She took a deep breath and wrote, "Two: Research criteria for success for location managers. Kick ass." After writing this step, she instinctively shielded the page so the kid in the Brown University sweatshirt wouldn't see the swear. As a location manager, she would learn more about set design, which would be an essential part of her overall knowledge; however, they already had the location, Jasper Equestrian.

What more is there to do?

On the paper, she continued, "Three: Take opportunities to go above and beyond. Impress." Each person she met would be another connection, another resource. Someone to impress or disappoint.

"Four: Figure out Margaret. Build a relationship." On this one, she paused. Because they had no real foundation, despite being related, getting to know Margaret would be like getting to know any other stranger.

Decades before, Olivia stood by the casket at her brother's funeral, the taste of wet salt at the corners of her mouth. Her uncle had stepped outside with the funeral director to finish their conversation about the error on the programs. Margaret approached Olivia and asked her how things were going in fifth grade. Margaret was the first person who didn't touch her on the face and say some version of, "Oh sweetie, I'm so sorry. This is *such* a tragedy."

Olivia stared up at her and said, "Everything is fine."

Margaret uncrossed her arms and responded, "Good girl. Work hard." And then she walked away. Olivia replayed those words for years because, despite the oddness she experienced in the moment, it was the first authentic piece of advice she received from an adult.

Good girl. Work hard.

Below this step, she wrote, "Five: Create documentary of life on set." She smiled at the idea. Having a project to work on meant she could use new skills in real-time and finish the experience with something tangible, a film of her own.

She glanced from the map toward the window and down at the topography. A river split the green land like the spine of a lizard. From above, the ground looked like home, familiar. She watched until she could make out a handful of swimming pools, a baseball field, and more open fields. She spotted the airfield just beyond the river. The plane landed with a thud, and Olivia's body tensed. It rolled forward, and she relaxed.

Finally, land.

Armed with a plan, she stepped off the plane and followed signs to baggage claim. The people looked like people do in airports, some tired and irritated, others ready to travel. Everyone was a stranger.

None of these people know me, and I know nothing about them.

While she waited for her bags, she stretched her legs and tried to crack her back, but it wouldn't pop. The dusty air scratched at her nose until she sneezed. A woman huffed insults under her breath, "Why does everything have to take so long?"

Olivia nodded in silent camaraderie.

She stepped to the side of the baggage carousel and opened the email to read the information for the rest of the day. "Take the C bus to Jasper Cliffs Center. Fellows should be in the meeting room on the first floor of the

Miller's Apartments by 4:30 p.m." She set an alarm on her phone for 4:15.

When her bags came, she piled her duffel onto her suitcase and adjusted the straps of the backpack on her aching shoulder. The essentials.

She searched for signs to Bus C, the one that would bring her to Jasper Cliffs Center. Around her, a line formed at a stand for Monarch Café. *Coffee would be nice.* She checked her watch: 2:47. Unsure of how long the bus would take, she skipped the coffee and went toward the exit.

When she stepped outside, hot wind blew into her face. She took off her sweatshirt and tied it around her waist. She wiped the sweat from her face and adjusted her bags.

The buses—A, B, and C—were lined like boxcars along the curb.

Olivia heaved her bags into the back of Bus C and found her seat. Her skin slid against the leather. She read the temperature gauge on the dash: 104. Sweat streaked down her back. *I hope there's time for a shower and a power nap.*

The engine stirred, and the bus rolled forward.

They drove down a highway for several minutes and pulled off at the Jasper Cliffs Center exit and then took a bridge above a river slightly larger than a creek. The roads turned, twisty and sharp. Her body vibrated as they passed over a bumpy section. She felt as if she were traveling down the spine of a lizard itself.

The chill of the air conditioner on sweat made her shiver. Goosebumps prickled on her skin. She untied her sweatshirt and pulled her arms through the sleeves. The roads shifted to the clear grid pattern that she had been expecting from her perusal of the map. *Thank goodness.*

For a town with the name of Jasper Cliffs, it sure was flat. The streets were lined with small shops and run-down buildings. Houses were set back from the road. The farther north they drove, the farther apart the buildings were spread.

When they pulled up at Jasper Cliffs Center bus station a few blocks later, each building had its own block.

Olivia read the map. The Miller's Apartments were only two blocks away.

Olivia eyed the dusty brick building. It stood four stories tall, and the brick crumbled in places. On the corner of the building, a flag waved. Monarch Café.

She stepped toward the front of the apartment building and pulled the door open. Greeted by an eggy stench, she blocked her nose and breathed through her mouth, but she could still taste it.

"Been dealing with a sulfur issue. Shouldn't be much longer we have to put up with that smell," a man wearing a navy suit jacket and dark jeans approached her and held out his hand.

She nodded and accepted the dry handshake.

"Noah Sherman," he said. "And you must be Olivia Gabriel. Everyone else is already here. Welcome home." He wiped droplets of sweat from his forehead with a handkerchief. "We pride ourselves here on offering a home for saints at an affordable rate. I heard you're a teacher. Teachers are saints. Plus, I'd do anything for Margaret." He winked. He ran his hand through shaggy, mustard colored hair. By the gray sprinkled throughout and the deepening wrinkles at his eyes and cheeks, she figured he must be in his early fifties. "I'll show you to your apartment. Follow me."

"It's good to be here. Thank you," she said nervously. This would be her home for the next six weeks. She adjusted the strap of the duffel on her aching shoulders.

"This building used to be a factory. My father restored it," Noah said proudly. "You're going to love it here. The first-floor offices are just down the hall a little further. The brick is original to the building," he said.

Smells original.

"The office Margaret rents from me is right down there," he said, pointing. "I assume that's where you'll be meeting her later." He led her into the elevator. "Do you have any questions for me?"

Olivia's body begged her to sit. She leaned against the wall of the elevator. The rotten egg smell lingered there too.

Olivia smiled. "No, I think I'm good." The building was simple. The first floor held offices and a fitness area; the other three floors, residences.

The elevator beeped, and they stepped out on the second floor. Noah led her to room 203. His enthusiasm for the place didn't seem to match the quality of the building. The paint peeled in places like someone had keyed the walls.

"All of our apartments are keyless entry. You just type your code into this keypad and turn the exterior lock. You'll never have to worry about forgetting your keys!" He sounded like a car salesman telling her about a fancy radio system. "Your code is 1234. There's a card inside with directions for how to reset it."

She followed his direction and typed in the four digits. She turned the lock and opened the door to the kitchen and living space.

"I'll leave you here. If you need anything, you can call the office. Numbers are on the paper on the fridge. If you need coffee or a snack, I highly recommend you stop by the original Monarch Café down on the first floor. Adira makes a great latte!"

Olivia smiled and nodded. "Thank you."

She dragged her bags through the open kitchen and living room and down the short hallway to the middle of the single bedroom on the right. Home for the next six weeks. She unpacked a few mismatched kitchen supplies, her pillow, a few outfits, and her camera equipment.

From her backpack, she procured the two framed five-by-seven-inch watercolor paintings of cardinals that her grandfather had painted and left Olivia in his will. She couldn't leave them behind; they meant too much to her. She set them on the windowsill.

After a refreshing hot shower in a decent bathroom, she laid down on the soft twin bed. Paint frayed from the ceiling in the shape of tiny icicles. Aside from the steady *whish* of air coming from the vents, everything was still. She relaxed onto the pillow and closed her eyes.

Seconds later, shouts came from the apartment above hers. She strained to make out the words, but they were muffled. It sounded like an argument. A door slammed. Then came the weeping. A woman. Olivia squeezed her eyes shut.

I hope she's okay.

Settling into a new place was one thing, but settling into a new life was another. Olivia took a deep breath and slid her hands under the pillow.

Settle, settle.

CHAPTER 10

Tick, tick, tick. The standard-issue clock matched the rhythm of her heart beating in her chest.

It was 4:05 p.m. In twenty-five minutes, she would meet the other fellows. In twenty-five minutes, she would see Margaret again. In twenty-five minutes, she would learn how this life would go. She would have a better sense of whether or not there was hope for a person like her in this industry.

She checked her backpack. Notebook. Pens. Camera. "We got this," she said to the cardinals. "Don't we?" The newness of it all threatened to overwhelm her. She could get used to the place. The apartment was basic and clean despite the peeling paint. Things were mostly quiet. But the people, she wondered, would she get along with the people? What would they be like? She exhaled.

"What are we forgetting?" She looked around to confirm she hadn't missed something, and then she left the apartment. Before going downstairs, she followed the directions left by Noah and reset the door code. *Safety first.*

She followed signs to the meeting room.
You got this.

As she approached the entrance, voices came from inside the room. She paused. Her nervous system awoke to the fact that she had to meet at least four new people in the next few minutes. She swallowed.

Be cool.

She stood up taller, straightened her shirt, and entered the room. Light streamed through industrial-sized windows.

"Olivia! Come in. Find the seat with your nametag and lanyard," Margaret said. She wore a bright pink blazer and a string of pearls.

Olivia found her spot at the far end of the oval table. The room was empty aside from the table and chairs and a few cardboard boxes. Nothing hung from the brick walls except a whiteboard.

"This is Jara. Jara, this is Olivia," Margaret said.

The woman sitting before her didn't need an introduction. Jara Jacobs. Last season's runner-up of the TV show *Surviving the Wilderness*. When the show aired, Olivia devoured it. At the end of the season, when the producers interviewed Jara after the show, she had said, "Time to pursue my big, big dream of writing and directing movies."

Me too, girl.

"Nice to meet you," Olivia said.

"Likewise," Jara said warmly. She sat with perfect, stick-straight posture and a pen pressed to the side of her cheek.

Margaret turned to Jara. "Now, what was your question again?"

Jara swept a dark brown hair out of her face and leaned down at her notebook.

Olivia examined the pile of items before her on the table: a tablet, folder, and walkie-talkie.

Wow. Cool.

She hung the lanyard with the nametag around her neck. *Olivia Gabriel, location manager.* Putting it on, she felt important. Proud.

"Haisley and Paige should be here shortly," Margaret said. As she finished speaking, two women entered the room. One of them held a pie.

"Hi, I'm Haisley. Pronounced *hazy* with the letter L inside," the blonde woman said cheerfully. "I hope you all like pecan pie."

Jara stood from her chair. "Let me help you with that," she said, taking the stack of plates from underneath Haisley's arm.

"It's so nice to meet everyone." Haisley beamed. She set the pie down in the center of the table and took her seat next to Margaret.

Paige, a mousy woman with corkscrew curls, nodded hello and took the final seat.

"Thank you, Haisley. This will be a great treat to end our meeting," Margaret said. "Welcome, everyone; I'm so glad you're all here. Welcome, officially, to the Roark Fellowship."

Haisley whooped as she took a sparkly pink notebook from her oversized purse. "This is so exciting!"

Olivia followed suit, taking her notebook from her backpack.

"No one told me I needed to bring a notebook," Paige said in a low voice.

Olivia opened hers, folded the page on the perforation, and tore out two pages. "Here you go," she said, sliding the pages to her new friend.

Paige brightened momentarily until something akin to worry appeared on her face. "Do you have an extra pen?"

Olivia nodded. A little skip of joy passed through her at the ability to help. She took a pen out of the compartment at the front of her backpack. "You can keep it."

"Thanks," Paige said, smiling slightly.

Margaret continued, "Jara, Paige, Haisley, Olivia. Ladies. To begin, I want you to think for a moment. How many times have you finished watching a movie or TV show and actually paid attention to the credits as they roll?"

Olivia smiled knowingly.

"Tonight, I want you to choose a show and fast-forward to the end, stop at the credits, and look at the names. Notice what you notice. I dream that more of those names are yours. Not just your names. I want those credits to be miles long with the names of women."

Olivia grinned. A dream rekindled.

"Let's go around the table. Let us know who you are and what you hope to get from this experience. Let's start with you, Haisley."

"I live upstairs with my husband, Al. We've been here for our whole lives. Al's a detective in the city, and I've been working in advertising. I heard about this opportunity on social media when Jasper Equestrian was tagged, and I knew I had to apply. I hope we all have a great time together and learn a lot."

"Yes, I'm sure we all will learn a lot." Margaret smiled.

Jara spoke, "Nice to meet you, ladies. I'm an artist and outdoor enthusiast. I'm working toward being a director, and I also love to write. Happy to be here."

Five pairs of eyes turned in Olivia's direction.

"Hi—hi, everyone," Olivia stuttered. "I'm Olivia. I graduated with a bachelor's in film and taught middle school for the last ten years."

She scanned the faces of the other women, looking for a curled lip of disapproval or a good-for-you nod, but none came—just a bunch of hard-to-read eyes.

"I'm looking forward to this opportunity and hope to learn as much as possible." She trailed to a stop, unsure if she should say more. What else could she say? She had zero *actual* experience. She glanced around at the faces of the other women, all around her age. If they found out about her relationship with Margaret, would they be upset? She didn't say anything more.

Margaret nodded and looked toward Paige.

"Hi, I'm Paige. I've been working with a major studio as a camera operator," she said flatly. "I'm here because I've been finding it hard to move up, and I hope to be a cinematographer someday."

Olivia made a mental note, *Mousey Paige. Cameras.*

Olivia's hand ached. She hadn't moved her fingers from their clenched spot beneath her thigh since she sat down. She adjusted and took a slow breath.

Margaret stood and held a tablet to demonstrate how they would use it. "Glad you're all here. Now for the details. As you know, you'll be working on my show, *Murder in Morristown*. We're in the second season of the show. It's about a series of murders that happen in the community of Morristown." Margaret directed them to open the call sheets on the tablets. "You'll find all the information you need in here to prepare for each day on set. Now let me tell you about the location."

Olivia perked up. *My domain.*

"The fictional town is run by the mayor who lives with his wife on a family ranch. Jasper Equestrian, as Haisley mentioned, down the street from here is the perfect setting for filming this. It's a horse ranch with indoor and outdoor filming locations. We'll use the stables, grounds, and the main house. There's a lot to work with here."

Olivia took notes as Margaret spoke.

"Beginning tomorrow, you'll meet at Jasper at six in the morning to start the day. Bring a water bottle, lanyards and tablets, and anything else you need to do your jobs. You'll be able to get there using golf carts since there's a dirt path between here and there. Keys are on your lanyards with the number of the cart you've been assigned. Olivia, you'll get there first, about five-thirty, since you'll help your mentor let everyone onto the set. Cool?"

Olivia nodded enthusiastically.

"On the first day, wear your shirts," Margaret continued, holding a bright, lime green T-shirt with "Roark Fellowship" printed across the chest. "Your mentors will be able to easily spot you and give you the lay of the land. I want you to know how excited I am to have you here this season. We need you, whatever you do after this, and I'm glad you're here."

Olivia smiled.

"One more thing before we dig into this pie," Margaret said. She put her hands on her hips. "At the end of the fellowship, one of you will be offered a full-time spot on my team."

The women gasped.

This is my chance.

"Only one of us?" Paige asked.

"Only one of you," Margaret repeated. "I'll select one of you to be a full-time member of my staff. I'll be looking for the person who works the hardest and complements my style the best."

The women exchanged glances, assessing the competition.

"Now, let's have some pie."

Haisley stood and cut the pie as Jara held out plates and passed slices around the table. Olivia gave a plate to Paige.

"Can't eat nuts," said Paige, frowning. She passed the plate to Margaret.

Olivia soaked in the sweet, starchy smell as she took a bite. Nothing good came easily, but she was up for a challenge.

CHAPTER 11

Despite staying up most of the night reading call sheets, studying briefs, and memorizing the map of Jasper Equestrian, at the sound of her alarm, Olivia leapt out of bed. She fumbled through the darkness and switched on the light. There were things to do to prepare. She started with a refreshing plunge in a cold shower and dressed in the neon T-shirt.

In the living room, she unzipped her backpack and loaded the tablet and notebook into the bag. She took the camera battery off the charger and put it back into its case. She scratched her chin. *What am I forgetting?*

She went back into the bedroom and looked around. The lanyard and badge were draped next to the cardinal paintings on the windowsill. "Whoops," she said, swinging it over her head. "Okay, here we go."

Outside, Olivia peered in the darkness toward the parking lot across the street while the rest of the world slept. She found #3, her assigned golf cart, and wiped pine needles off the seat. She secured her backpack and camera bag beside her and started the cart.

She turned on the headlights and steered out of the lot and down the dirt path. Her body vibrated, and she gripped the wheel. With the light from the headlights, she could see where she was going, and with all the trees on either side of her, there was nowhere to turn. It was as if she were in a tunnel.

She came to a clearing where the path met a road. Across the street, two black metal gates supported a steel banner that read, "JASPER EQUESTRIAN," like the entrance to an amusement park.

She pulled up to the call box where she could request access. On one side of the screen, there was a small reflection of Olivia; on the other, a choice—enter a code or press the fat green call button.

She smiled, unsure of who might be watching her on the other end. Every time she stood in front of the security camera at school, she felt awkward and nervous. This was the same. She pressed the green button and waited.

She checked her watch. At 5:30 a.m., the place was dark and still. According to Margaret, all the horses would be gone during the week while filming happened. She pressed the button again and heard a buzzing sound.

"Olivia?" a voice asked.

She knew from Margaret that her mentor would be waiting. "Yes, I'm here." Her voice cracked at its first use.

"Opening the gate as we speak. Drive straight back and park in front of the stables on the right."

The gates swung backward, and Olivia stepped on the gas. She drove toward the stables and stopped at a poster-sized sign that read, "Crew Parking." Olivia took in the enormity of the place. The main house, practically a mansion, sat regally on the land, giant compared to every other house Olivia had seen so far in Jasper Cliffs.

As she gathered her bags from the cart, a voice rose behind her.

"Olivia, it's so nice to see you again! I'm so excited to get started." Noah stood before her.

"Hey Noah, Margaret said I should be here now to meet my mentor."

"Yes, indeedy. You're looking at him," he said, pointing two thumbs toward his chest. "You, Olivia Gabriel, are the luckiest fellow in the group."

Oh boy.

"Follow me," Noah said as he strolled forward with his hands in the pockets of dark blue jeans.

She followed him down a path past the stables to the front lawn of the main house.

"The stables are one of the main filming locations we'll use for several shots this season. Have you reviewed the call sheet for today?"

Olivia pretty much had it memorized. The crew call would be at six, and the first shot of the day would start at eight. They would break for breakfast at ten and then start shooting again at eleven. Lunch at two. Then more shooting. Today's scenes would be shot in front of the house, and no extras would be needed. "Yep, I reviewed it."

"Awesome." Noah stopped in the middle of the path. The property around them stretched in all directions. "From here, you can see almost everything. The front of the house will be a great backdrop. Then toward the east, you get a good view of the land and the stables. Crew parking, as you saw, is near the entrance. The only thing you can't see from here is production. They'll be set up in trailers behind the house."

Olivia nodded. "What about meals? I read in the notes I should meet the caterers. Where does that happen?"

"We'll have catering set up breakfast and lunch on the plastic tables in the yard over there," he said, pointing to an open space on the east side of the house. "Monarch Café does our meals, but I'll have you place the orders. I'll show you all of that today."

Olivia's mental list grew longer, but she could handle it. "Sounds great."

Noah started walking again, and Olivia went alongside him.

"First thing first, letting everyone through the gates. Let's go inside, and I'll show you what to do."

Inside the house, Noah led her through a living room, down a hallway, and into a room with a sign on the door that read, "Loc. Mgr. Office." Noah took a seat in an office chair at a desk. He pulled out a folding chair and gestured for Olivia to sit.

A flatscreen computer monitor showed the area outside the gate.

"Everyone who comes in should show you their badge, and you can buzz them in by pressing here." He pointed to a matching green button on the screen. "No one has the numerical code to the gate except for Margaret and me, but we'll give that to you so that after today you can let yourself in if we're not here yet."

"Sounds great."

"I have a couple of things going on in other places, so I'll be in and out. If you need me, you can call me on the walkie. We'll all be on station one. Production is on two."

Olivia set it to station one.

"There's still some time if you want to go down to the kitchen to grab a cup of coffee before people start arriving. I'll meet you again outside at six."

Noah left, and Olivia pulled the tablet out of her bag. She scanned the call sheet, but there was nothing new to learn. The smell of coffee lured her to the kitchen. She poured a cup and brought it back to her office. She wrapped her hands around the Styrofoam cup and stared at the screen.

Mornings at school were never this calm.

This is kind of nice.

At school, she would run from the copy machine to the kitchen to the classroom and back again. Another teacher would pop into the room and ask a question, and she'd forget to refill her water bottle. She'd be thirsty, but at least she wouldn't need to go to the bathroom.

She breathed in the slow quiet until a car appeared on the monitor.

One after another, Olivia buzzed people into set. Some arrived in golf carts, others in cars. A few minutes after six, the walkie talkie beeped. "All crew report to the front lawn."

This is it. Don't get scared now.

Shaking out the jitters, Olivia left the office and went outside. A woman with lean, chiseled arms called for everyone to gather around. She had a buzzcut and high cheekbones. "Hi, all. I'm JD the AD," she chuckled, "AD, the first assistant director."

Olivia looked admiringly at JD. *Badass.*

"Welcome to the new crew members. We're glad to have you. We only have a couple of notes this morning, and then you can get to work." JD's hawkish eyes peered across the group. "Set your walkie channel to one. Don't be late. Ask for help. Fellows, stick with your mentors."

The fellows nodded. Who had the other women been paired with?

"For this week's rotation, we'll have each of you observe one scene to see how Margaret works, otherwise you'll focus on learning the ropes of your primary roles with your mentors. Starting next week, we'll have one of you acting as an assistant director with me each week for the final four weeks of filming. This will give you direct exposure and a glimpse of what it would be like to do this full-time. You'll know your week from your assignments on the call sheet. Let's get to work."

Everyone scattered. Olivia searched the group for Noah. *Where is he?* Paige searched for her mentor too.

"You'll be with me," JD said to Paige. "Your mentor had to go home. Family emergency. But I was told you have camera experience, so I'll get you set up. Just give me a minute."

"Cool," Paige said.

Paige had basically been promoted to a lead job on the first day.

"Are you excited?" Olivia asked Paige.

"Yes, I am. And I'm a little nervous too. Not sure what to expect, you know? We'll see. But yes. Sorry, that wasn't clear. I know I tend to ramble when I talk. I'm excited! How about you?" Her voice squeaked like windshield wipers in a drizzly summer rain.

"Yeah, I am too," Olivia said in an upbeat voice, trying to mask the jealousy she was feeling. "I'll see you later."

Olivia went inside and found Noah huddled at the computer in the office. "What's up, kid? Ready to do this?"

Kid? She felt unsettled with him calling her that even if he was twenty years older, but she said, "Yep, I'm ready." She opened her tablet and followed Noah's guidance as he taught her the key tasks she would complete.

"Catering orders are submitted on Monday for the following week. If someone from Monarch has questions for you, they'll come to the office. I'll introduce you to them today."

Olivia added the task to her calendar.

"Aside from food, the big thing for you will be keeping the location information updated on the call sheets. This is the main place for everyone involved in filming to get their info, so it needs to be accurate. That includes the parking info, weather, meal schedule, and when it's your turn for a rotation as AD, you'll also update the special instructions for the crew with the scene notes for set dressing, sound, and props."

Olivia leaned over the tablet, following along. Ready.

Margaret came into the office, brushing disheveled hair off her face. "Hey you two. I might need a favor." She wore gray cargo shorts and a black T-shirt. A checkered bandana hung loosely around her neck.

Noah frowned. "What's up?"

Margaret closed the door and pulled open the third folding chair, joining them at the table. "We're filming the first murder scene today, and Brian's not feeling well." Her voice was gruff and serious.

Noah and Margaret exchanged worried glances.

The lead actor not feeling well can't be good.

Noah pulled at the gray hairs on his chin. "That kid is so sensitive. What do you want to do?"

Margaret looked around the room. "I'm thinking this is more a case of nerves than anything else. Let's give him some time. Maybe a cup of tea?"

"I'll go talk to him," Noah said. "Man to man."

Margaret's eyes flickered.

"Nothing against you," he added.

Margaret and Noah held eye contact for a moment. Then Margaret turned her attention to Olivia. "I need to meet with Tiffany about her part. Can you do me a favor and ride back to the office at Miller's and get my purse? I forgot it on the back of the door."

"Of course," Olivia rose from the chair.

"And while you're there, grab me a latte from Monarch." She curled her lips in disgust as she looked down at the paper cup of coffee on the table. "I can't drink this."

Olivia nodded. While she didn't want to miss any of the action on the set, she was glad to have a way to help Margaret.

"Gate code is 052811 for when you come back," Margaret said in a near whisper. "Don't give that code to anyone else. It stays between you, me, and Noah. Property owner's instructions and safety, obviously. Not like anything would ever happen in a small town like this."

"Of course. I'm on it," Olivia said. She picked up the keys and left the room, part of the team.

CHAPTER 12

Success that morning meant fulfilling Margaret's request, but Olivia couldn't help but wonder what she would miss back on set.

She started the golf cart. Behind her, the set bustled with activity. Lights squeaked as Haisley and her mentor, Fizz, the bald-headed gaffer, got them into position.

Olivia drove off the property and across the street. The set noise faded until all she could hear was the crunch of dirt beneath her and the rumble of the cart. An endless repetition of pine trees guided her forward.

She pressed harder on the gas. The sun was barely above the horizon, and the heat weighed heavy on her already.

When she reached the lot, she parked the cart and went back into the building. She found the office, unlocked the door, and turned on the light. Margaret's turquoise purse hung from a hook on the back of the door. Olivia took the purse off the hook and draped the stringy thing around her neck like a sash so that she would be able to carry the drinks.

Inside the café, she felt a refreshing blast from the air conditioner and soaked in the aroma of freshly ground coffee beans. A few people sat at tables, and a fit man in workout clothes stood with his arms crossed. The art on the walls, paintings in brilliant yellows and greens, reminded Olivia of an art gallery.

Olivia stared down at the drink list taped to the counter. Had Margaret told her what kind of drink to buy? Latte? Americano? *Something fancy*, she remembered.

When she looked up, she was startled by the beautiful dark eyes of the barista. Something stirred within her. The woman, a silver stud in her nose, smiled. "What can I get for you today?"

Olivia's hands got clammy, and her heart fluttered.

The woman brushed a strand of hair, fallen from the chestnut-colored messy bun, off her face. She had something gray, speckles, on the black shoulder of the T-shirt she wore beneath the apron. Her name, Adira, was pinned to her chest in capital letters.

Olivia felt the strap of the purse around her neck. *Why am I wearing this awkward turquoise purse?*

"Can I please have a latte and an iced coffee?" she asked.

"Absolutely." Adira punched some keys, and Olivia fumbled for her debit card. "I'll have it for you at the end of the counter."

Olivia stepped to the end of the counter. She played with the thin rubber key chain, pulling it from her wrist, twisting and untwisting it between her fingers, slowly, like rolling dough in strands for pasta. She searched for something to say, but emptiness and lousy pickup lines she would never say aloud were the only thoughts that came to her mind. She imagined herself saying something quick like, "You into me?" and chuckled to herself at how bizarre the words sounded in her mind and how funny they would feel coming out of her mouth.

Behind the counter, Adira dripped steaming milk over the top of the espresso. Her hand moved in slow, steady circles high above the cup, stirring feelings in Olivia. It had been a while since she felt this sensation, light and airy.

Adira walked toward Olivia, grinning, and handed her two paper cups. Black ink peeked from beneath the sleeves of her shirt; the phases of the moon dripped down her arm.

"You like it?" Adira asked, looking down at the lattes.

Very much. Two perfectly symmetrical flowers stared up at her. "It's v, v cute," she said. "Nice artwork." As soon as the words came out, Olivia wanted to slam her palm into her forehead.

Speak in whole words, you goof.

Adira frowned and wiped her hands on the apron. "I totally got your order wrong, didn't I?"

Still looking at the flowers, Olivia lied, "This is exactly what I wanted."

Adira smiled shyly and twirled a strand of chestnut hair between her fingers.

"Thank you," Olivia said. She pressed down the lid, and hot liquid dripped on her knuckles. She licked it away.

"See you around," Adira said.

It took twice as long to get back to set with the drinks bobbing in the cup holder. Sweat trickled down Olivia's forehead. She entered the code at the gate and drove forward, parking the cart. Margaret and Noah stood with Brian in front of the trailers.

Wow, a real actor. Be cool.

She held out the latte and uncurled the purse from around her neck.

"Thank you," Margaret said, taking the cup and purse from Olivia.

"Anything else?" Olivia asked.

"We're all set," Margaret said, raising her hand in a brushing manner.

"Are you sure?" Olivia lingered. She had never been asked to do a favor for a director of an actual television show before. Another one might give her more points toward a full-time offer.

Margaret's eyes flickered over Brian as if she were assessing his wellbeing. Brian stood tall and sipped long drags of tea from a Styrofoam cup.

"We're good," Noah said. "Head over and join the other fellows in front of the house. You're all going to observe the first shot. We'll be right there."

Olivia studied Margaret and Noah. She had a finely tuned pride-o-meter that let her assess how a person felt about her on a scale of disappointed to proud. Margaret's eyes, still fixed on Brian, hadn't registered on the meter at all. Noah hovered somewhere around neutral.

Olivia shrugged. She walked down the path toward the place in the lawn where the crew was setting up. Filming outside required equipment adjustments. Olivia watched closely, learning. Haisley adjusted the light stands. Fizz followed behind her the whole time like a dad behind a toddler on their first bike ride.

JD the AD called the fellows together and said, "Make sure you stay quiet during each take. Between takes, you can observe anything that's going on—our conversations with the actors, lighting adjustments, minor set changes—but try to stay in the background. Jara, you stay with me."

Olivia stood next to Paige so that she could see the shot. Paige squinted into the camera, setting up.

Brian joined them and took his position between the camera and lights with Tiffany, his costar.

Margaret directed everyone to quiet down for the first take. Noah stood next to her with his arms crossed.

"Action," Margaret called.

Brian walked a few steps, and Paige turned the camera so that it moved with him. He bent down and picked up the newspaper. The camera zoomed in on the paper, catching the headline. "Six-year-old grieves the death of her mother."

Brian's lip quivered.

"Cut!" Margaret called.

Olivia moved closer to Margaret so that she could hear.

"Nice first take, Brian, but it's coming off a little too sad. You're remorseful, but only for a fraction of a second. As soon as you feel your lip quiver, turn it into a smirk and continue your conversation with Tiffany. Tiffany, excellent job. Don't change a thing. Let's try it again."

Brian nodded and went back into position. Tiffany uncrossed her arms and reset her smile.

"Take two."

Brian did the same motion. This time, his lip didn't quiver at all.

"Cut!"

Margaret and Brian met again.

"Okay, let's regroup," Margaret said. "Remember, you're playing a serial killer. On that take, it felt more like a kindergarten teacher. You'll be remorseful for a second, and then you'll smirk. You don't really feel guilty."

Sweat dripped down Brian's handsome, scruffy face, and JD handed him a towel. He wiped his face. "All these women that you brought are making it hard for me to concentrate."

Margaret scanned the group. "Let's have everyone take ten steps back."

The crew retreated.

They ran the scene a couple more times, and Margaret called "cut" each time. Olivia scratched her chin. It seemed as if Margaret was looking for something that no one else could see.

Margaret shook her head. She spoke to Brian and Tiffany, "This shot isn't working for me. Brian, we need to get this one right for your character to stay relatable."

With a flick of her finger, Margaret motioned for Noah to come toward her. She whispered something in his ear.

No one else moved. Curiosity anchored Olivia to the ground. *How will Margaret handle this?*

Margaret spoke to Brian, "What the producer and the fans love about this show is your character. When I'm watching you now, it seems like you're not here, and not in the way that would be good ambivalence. I don't see the passion in your eyes that I saw when I watched the films of the first season. I don't feel the emotion."

Brian nodded and rubbed his upper lip with the back of his hand.

Olivia bit her lip. Margaret knew what to say and how to say it. *How did she learn how to do that?*

"Let's take a short break. Back in five," Margaret said.

Noah went to Brian and the two of them stepped off to the side. Margaret observed with desperate eyes.

Brian shook his head and said to Noah, "There are so many people. I know I'm messing up, and just feeling so many eyes on me is making it worse."

Noah nodded. "What's getting in your way of doing this well?"

"It's hard to connect with a character who plays a serial killer."

"What do you need in order to get it right?"

"Maybe I need to kill someone," Brian said, laughing.

"That's not a bad idea. Just don't kill me," Noah joked, relieving the tension in the group.

Olivia shuddered.

Death.

Death was something that ran through her mind like a TV left on in the background. There was a game she used to play with the neighbors in a backyard pool. The kids would swim under the water and grab each other by the ankles and pull each other down. She never liked the game, but she played along.

One day when she was seven, she sat in a chair outside of the pool with a *Lion King* towel over her shoulders, eating a green freeze-pop, when she saw one of the girls in the water pull another by the ankle. The girl being dragged down was laughing, and when she went under, she choked on some water. Young Olivia watched the girl coughing, pushing and pulling the water but unable to breathe. Olivia let out a single yelp but no one came; she was frozen on the sidelines. By the time the older kids got her out of the pool, it was too late.

Olivia tried to talk to her mom about what had happened. A single tear crawled down Olivia's cheek as her mom said, "What are you crying for? Nothing happened to you, did it?" Olivia wiped the tear, and that ended the discussion, but it was only the beginning of the guilt. She told herself that if anyone was ever in danger, this time she would know how to respond.

The only thing they were in danger of now was not getting a good shot.

Margaret, off to the side, relaxed her face, smiling slightly at the two guys. *Sometimes leadership is knowing when to step back*, Olivia figured.

Olivia pulled her camera out of its bag and took a few shots of the actors on set. Noah patted Brian on the shoulder and sent him back to his mark with a go-get-'em shove. Then he strode out of the stable.

With the camera, Olivia panned to Margaret and JD, who chatted with their hands on their hips, arms reddening in the sun. Brian paced back and forth. Behind the water cooler, Tiffany drank from a plastic bottle.

Margaret walked back to Brian and said, "You got this."

"Let's go, everyone," JD called. "Sixty second warning. Take your places."

Olivia put the camera away and took her spot among the crew. On the next take, Margaret didn't call cut until after Tiffany finished her lines, and everyone high-fived. With a victory under their belt, Margaret announced the first break.

A message appeared on Olivia's tablet from Noah: "Meet me at the food area ASAP."

CHAPTER 13

When she arrived in front of the catering van, her heart nearly stopped. A warm sizzle spread through her stomach, and she tried to hide the smile that was spreading across her face.

"Olivia, this is Adira. Adira, Olivia," Noah said.

Olivia and Adira exchanged smiles. "Hey," Olivia said, flicking a piece of hair behind her ear. She set down her backpack and camera bag beside the catering van.

"Nice to see you," Adira said, eyes dancing in the sunlight.

Inside Olivia, a marching band played. A cool breeze blew, and she took a deep breath.

Olivia tried to concentrate as Noah spoke, "Adira or someone on her team will bring the meals for breakfast and lunch and will set them up here. Adira, if you need anything, Olivia will be in the office, or you can text her. I'll let you swap numbers and take it from here." Noah walked away.

Olivia bit her lip.

"It's great to see you again," Adira said. They stood by the van while the cast and crew made their way through the food line.

"You too," Olivia smiled. She reached for her phone, and Adira recited her number. Olivia typed the number and sent a text message: "This is Olivia Gabriel."

"So, Olivia Gabriel, you work here?" Adira asked. Her voice hummed, and she smelled like vanilla and coffee.

"I'm here for a fellowship and possibly a full-time role working on the show if all goes well." Olivia grinned. All had been going well so far, and she could see herself succeeding.

"Congratulations. I hope it all goes well." Adira smiled.

Olivia pulled at the skin underneath her fingernails. *What do I say?*

Her fears came rushing back. She heard Gina's voice saying, "You're so awkward. You never do anything."

She choked out the words, "Do you need anything now? Otherwise, I should get back to work."

"I'm all set. Thank you, though. I'll see you later?" Adira's smile, warm and electric, sent a tingling sensation through Olivia.

She grinned, nodded, and shuffled back to the filming area.

"That's a wrap," Margaret called to the crew a few minutes before six.

People scattered like ants until Olivia found herself alone. She turned on her camera to review the footage she had shot in her spare moments that day. She scanned the videos for moments of truth, authenticity.

"With so much *acting* going on," she laughed to the camera, "it's hard to capture the truth."

She replayed the moment she had captured earlier in the day between takes. In the shot, Brian pushed

Margaret's hand off his shoulder. *Intense, that's good.* But she had been so far away, the footage was blurry. "We can do better," she said to the camera.

Olivia walked toward the food area where people pulled slices of pizza from boxes. Margaret headed toward the parking area with Jara. Olivia moved to catch up with them, eager for feedback about how she was doing so far. She stopped. What did she do all day except things Margaret probably wouldn't even notice?

She turned and went back. She collected empty plastic bottles and put them in a recycling bin. As the location manager, part of her job was to ensure the place was clean at the end of each day. Tasks like this were fine; there was something satisfying to her about being able to cross them off her to-do list. Still, her legs ached, and her lower back begged her to sit.

She picked up another bottle as Haisley strode toward her. Blonde hair sprung from dark roots that made a straight line down the center of her head.

"Need any help?" Haisley asked.

"I'm good," Olivia said. "Just grabbing these last few bottles, cleaning off the table, and then I'll be close to finishing things here." Olivia turned to pick up another bottle and sensed Haisley behind her.

"Do you want to hang out on Friday night? I'd love to have you and the other fellows over for dinner. You should come if you want to. We all live in the apartments, so it won't be a big to-do. Bring leftovers from the set if you want." Haisley's voice was soft and kind.

Remnants of pizza crust and crumbling cookies lay scattered across the table. The handwritten sign reading,

"Take what you want, leave the rest," hung by a single piece of blue painter's tape.

Dinner with the women would be nice.

"Sure, I'd love to come," Olivia said, and it was mostly the truth. Friends, actual friends, would be a good thing. At the same time, she needed to focus on her job. And to do it well, she would need to work off set too. There wouldn't be too much time to socialize. People like Haisley didn't understand that. But she also needed relationships.

"Great! Yay for the weekend!" Haisley cheered. "How's everything else going?"

"Pretty well," Olivia said. "How about you?"

"So far, all good," Haisley said. "Are you happy with your mentor?"

Olivia tossed another bottle into the recycling bin, sending her mind to the last day of school with her students. It felt like a lifetime had passed since then.

"Noah seems pretty cool," Haisley said when Olivia didn't respond.

"Yeah, I'm happy," Olivia said in an unconvincing tone. Noah hadn't done much yet. Aside from telling her what to do, he hadn't given her any advice. The mentoring would probably come after she had the basics down. "How about you?"

Haisley frowned. "I'm not sure about Fizz yet. He's always right behind me. I get the sense he's not used to taking a backseat." She shrugged. "We'll see. I'm going to head out. Monday is margarita night. I'll see you tomorrow." She swung her bright pink bag over her shoulder and walked toward the carts.

After cleaning the food table and checking the place one more time for anything out of place, Olivia drove out of Jasper Equestrian and stopped on the other side of the gate. She stepped out of the cart. The temperature had gone down significantly, cooling the steel gate. She wiggled the bars to make sure it clicked shut. Finding it locked, she got back in the cart and drove back to the apartments.

CHAPTER 14

By the end of the first week, Olivia had a firm grasp of the primary filming locations. That was a good thing, too, because she had no idea where Noah was half the time. Earlier that morning, he wandered away muttering something about needing to finish payroll for one of the other properties he managed.

In the small office, Olivia folded her legs on the swiveling chair. Bare feet pressed into her thighs, she watched people arrive at the gate and as they approached, she pressed the button for entry. Members of the crew arrived in golf carts that they then parked along the back of the twenty-stall horse stable.

Cast and crew slipped from the back doors of all kinds of cars and walked through the gates as Olivia buzzed them in. If the vehicle was black and the windows tinted, it probably contained an actor. On the monitor, Olivia saw Margaret pull up in the glistening black BMW. *Nice wheels.* She pushed the button and watched Margaret drive through the gates.

Despite working together in this context, nothing had changed in their relationship.

Maybe I should try to talk to her more.

Margaret disappeared from the screen toward the primary filming location in front of the house. Margaret's vision, which she shared in-depth with the fellows, included several conflicts that happened in front of the house. "Poor people fighting in front of such a lovely home," she had said, using words like "juxtaposition" and "double entendre" in the same sentence.

Pins and needles ran from Olivia's right hand up to her shoulder. She switched to buzzing with her left hand. She yawned. The morning lull. She stretched her arms and used the moments between buzzing to review the schedule for the following week when the excitement would begin: her rotation as acting first assistant director.

She stood and shook out her legs. No cars or carts waited for her, so she went out into the hallway and down to the kitchen for a fresh cup of coffee. She moved between mingling crew members, making her way toward the coffeepot. She filled her thermos while nodding and saying good morning to a pair of guys drinking coffee by the sink. She recognized, and could sometimes name, most of the crew members.

The fellows, she knew. Jara was always at Margaret's heels saying something that made Margaret bob her head enthusiastically. Haisley on the lights. Camera, Paige.

Olivia took the coffee back to her spot in front of the monitors. The space in front of the gate was clear; no one was waiting for her.

Margaret poked her head in the door. "Hey, Olivia. Do you have a few minutes now to meet and run through things for next week?"

Coffee scalded the tip of Olivia's tongue. "Yes, I'm ready." She took a deep breath and picked up the tablet with the drafted call sheets for each day. She followed Margaret toward her office.

When Margaret opened the door to the office, Brian and Noah looked up at them from the table.

"Can you give us a minute? We're talking shop," Noah said.

Talking shop?

"Sure," Margaret said curtly.

Olivia and Margaret went back into the hallway. Noah closed the door.

"I'll be right with you," Margaret said to Olivia, walking away and down the hall toward the bathroom.

From outside the office, Olivia could hear the men discussing Brian's performance.

"I felt comfortable when Tim was our director. Somehow, it was easier," Brian said. "Tiffany nails her scenes every time. And I'm playing a *murderer* in this show. Do you know how fucking hard that is? The range that it requires..." Brian trailed off.

"You are doing fine, man," Noah said. "Continue to practice getting into character. Push yourself."

Olivia shook her head. Noah was a mentor, just not hers.

Margaret returned. "They're still in there?"

Olivia nodded.

"Let's go meet in the living room instead."

At the coffee table in the living room, Margaret pulled a stylus from behind her ear.

"Let's start with the first scene on Monday morning. We're going to do that shot in the stable. Then I'll have you prepare to help me with the scene out back after lunch. We might move to one final shot out front if we have time, but I'm not sure we'll get to that one."

As Margaret explained the scenes, all business, Olivia noted the details on the shot list. No one would ever guess they were related because she only ever discussed work. Olivia breathed a sigh of relief.

When she finished, Margaret said, "I've seen you observing everything. You seem to be soaking it all in. When it's your turn as the first AD, don't be afraid to speak up. If you see something that looks off, let me know."

Olivia beamed at the first piece of feedback. "Thank you. I will."

She spent the rest of the morning daydreaming about Monday. She rehearsed what she might suggest to Margaret: *This might be better if we shoot from another angle. We might want to consider changing the lighting.*

By lunchtime, the only thing she was hungry for was affirmation.

When the sun sagged in the west and then crawled behind the house, man-made lights, dozens of them, took their turn. The artificial lights stood guard around the place in an oval like a football stadium. The final scene of the week was being shot in front, and everyone was there.

Fizz circled Haisley as she adjusted one of the smaller lights behind the actors. "A little to the left," he said.

She moved it to the left.

"A little to the right," he said.

She stopped and glared at him. "Which is it?" Her voice was tight.

That's how I'd sound too, Olivia thought, *if I'd spent the whole week being micromanaged.*

Fizz examined the light with a hand on his bald chin. "Where you have it is fine," he said.

Actors milled around each other, rehearsing their lines into the air. The words fell on top of each other like a collapsing stack of Jenga bricks. Margaret stood with her arms crossed. Each minute on set cost hundreds of dollars. Margaret wouldn't let them forget it.

"Five-minute warning!" JD called to everyone through the megaphone.

Margaret leaned toward Jara and whispered something that Olivia couldn't hear. With her experience, Jara had an advantage. She conversed easily with Margaret, JD, and the others as if she'd worked with them for years.

Not fair.

Olivia picked at her fingernails and skimmed the notes for the scene. Even though the fellows were there to observe, she wanted to find something she might be able to say today: a preview for Margaret that she would add value to the show. Maybe something brilliant would appear in magic ink on the tablet in front of her, a gift from the universe.

Nothing came.

"We're not done yet. Get ready for the next take," Margaret instructed. Drooping crew members jumped to their feet and took their spots like athletes in a game, everyone knowing exactly where to go.

Olivia followed Margaret back toward the actors, saying a quick prayer to no one in particular that she would find the words to impress Margaret.

"We need to get this shot. Brian, you can do this. Go deep. Come on, buddy," Margaret coached. Margaret had been trying to get Brian to express emotions that Olivia wasn't sure men had ever had to feel. Remorse. Empathy.

Olivia trained her eye on Brian, who leaned over the most recent of his murder victims. His face strained over the lifeless actress.

"Cut!" Margaret called. "We'll go again in two."

Jara stepped in front of Olivia and said to Brian, "What if you try remembering a time when you felt bad about something that you did?"

Why didn't I think of that? Olivia scanned her notes in frustration and took a deep breath.

Brian stared at Jara and then looked at Margaret, his eye twitching.

Margaret turned to Brian. "It's a good idea, Brian. Why don't you try it?"

Brian opened his mouth to say something, but then stopped. Olivia felt something strange, as if she were watching a child who disagreed with their mother.

"Okay, let's do this again. Everyone, take your places," Margaret directed, and the scene sprung to life. Jara stood behind Margaret. Olivia hung behind Jara, leaning forward to see the scene. The actors broke into character.

"Cut," Margaret called. "This will be fine for now, and we can start again on Monday." She went to Brian and said, "Get some rest this weekend. Let's do one more take of this one on Monday."

Brian scowled and kicked the side of the door with the toe of his boot.

Yikes.

Margaret crossed her arms. "Everyone, go home and get some rest. We'll start with the next scene on Monday morning."

Olivia bent down and took out her camera to capture another shot of life on set. When Olivia stood up again, Haisley came by and said, "See you tonight for dinner?"

Olivia wanted to hang out with the women, but she also had a lot of work to do. Jara, the frontrunner, was a step ahead. Still, spending time with the women would be nice. She felt herself being pushed and pulled between career and friendships—two things that she wanted, but things that took time, attention, work, practice. She nodded. "I'll be there."

CHAPTER 15

Olivia pressed on the gas pedal until her foot couldn't go any lower. She leaned forward, gripping the steering wheel, willing it to move faster. "Come on, little cart," she urged. It reached its upper speed of twenty miles per hour.

She made a mental list. Shower. Black top. Jean shorts. Makeup. Birthstone necklace.

Her heart bounced in her chest as the golf cart bobbled forward along the dirt path.

She crossed out the list and started again. Shower. Blue shirt with stripes. Long jeans. No necklace.

Decisions.

She approached the lot, parked the cart in its spot, and hurried inside. The lingering smell of boiled eggs greeted her. She stopped to examine the row of silver mailboxes to find out where to go for dinner. There it was. Number 303. Al and Haisley Richards.

Apartment 303.

Would that mean Haisley lived in the apartment above hers?

She remembered the yells and sobs she had heard on the first afternoon when she arrived in Jasper Cliffs. Had they come from Haisley?

Sadness rose within her, thinking of Haisley in as much pain as the woman she had heard only a few nights before. Despite hoping she would do something if someone was in trouble and telling herself that she would, she hadn't done anything. Sadness turned to guilt.

She took the stairs two at a time to her apartment. She punched in the key code. In the doorway, she paused. Had she remembered to close the gate when she left Jasper? She sighed and mentally retraced her steps. Brian, her camera, Haisley's invite...

I must have.

She brushed the thought away as she tossed her camera bag and backpack on the floor by the couch and dashed to the bathroom to get ready. She showered and tried on four outfits before settling on the black top and jean shorts.

Thirty minutes later, she stuck her license and debit card in her pocket.

"Here goes nothing," she said to the cardinals and left the apartment.

She took the stairs to the third floor, walked down the gray hallway, and paused at the door of apartment 303.

"You know she's Roark's niece, right?" Olivia recognized the squeaky voice coming from inside the apartment.

"Are you serious?" Haisley asked.

Olivia froze with her fist in the air and let her arm fall gently back to her side.

"That's nepotism, right?" Paige squeaked. "I mean, I know Margaret's using a panel to pick the winner, but come on."

Olivia's stomach dropped. The words cut. She wrapped her arms across her body. She pictured a rubber duck floating at the top of a murky pool of ocean water. The duck wore a synthetic copy of Paige's bouncing, corkscrew curls. Its innocent smirk mocking the friendship Olivia thought they'd had.

For a moment, her mind went to the last day of school. To Isabel. Crying over the drawing she had likely worked so hard to create.

She sucked in a deep breath of air, hoping it would wash away the sadness stirring inside her.

It's fine. I'm fine.

Margaret's sharp eyes would be on her the following week during her rotation as first assistant director; Margaret would judge her work as she did everyone else. There was nothing more to their relationship no matter how much Olivia wished that were different. Did she really expect Paige to know all that?

The sound of footsteps came from behind her.

"You going to knock?"

Olivia turned around.

Jara stood with long athletic arms extended from the sleeves of a dark blue top. She unzipped her purse and painted dark maroon lipstick across her lips.

"Oh, yes, I was just…" Olivia started. Before she could finish a sentence, Jara reached for the door, rapping on the white space above the keypad with sturdy knuckles.

Olivia forced her cheeks to rise into a smile as the door opened.

"Welcome, ladies! Come on in," Haisley said. Haisley wore an oversized black T-shirt with the words "bad choices make good stories" printed on the front.

Olivia took an unsatisfying breath and stepped into the apartment.

The layout was identical to hers. Olivia's living area was bare; Haisley and Al's, packed. The room matched Haisley's personality—colorful. A leather couch sat across from a big-screen TV mounted onto the wall with a glittery frame. On the left side of the room stood a shelf with meticulously arranged prints in all colors. A smaller bookcase leaned against the wall on the right side of the room. It held three shelves of books and a pink ceramic bowl filled with coins and wine corks.

Olivia touched the smooth edge of the pea-sized sapphire stone hanging at her neck. *Maybe I shouldn't have worn this,* she thought, hoping they didn't think she was trying too hard.

"You ladies want a drink? How about a Mint Julep? Do you like whiskey?" Haisley asked, turning on music through the TV.

"Yes! That's what I'm talking about," Jara said.

"Whiskey's great," Olivia said, hoping it was true.

From the couch, Paige waved. Olivia forced a smile.

Haisley poured liquid from a pitcher into two glasses and stuck a sprig of mint on top.

"Cheers," Haisley said. "To a great night. Let's get to know each other." Haisley raised a glass, and the rest of the women followed.

Olivia stood at the counter and took a sip of the cool mint drink, letting it rinse away the bitterness of the day.

You can do this. Be cool.

The door opened, and a man dressed head to toe in neon athletic gear entered the apartment. Olivia blinked at the green-yellow fluorescence. Even his laces were a vibrant yellow.

"Ladies, this is my husband, Al," Haisley said, standing and walking toward him. "You've probably seen him biking around town or riding in his police cruiser."

"Nice to meet you all," he said, putting his bike helmet onto the windowsill. His teeth sparkled white. He had athletic shoulders and long arms.

"Nice to meet you," the women responded.

Jara joined Paige on the couch.

Olivia studied Al's face. The shouts replayed in her mind. His cheekbones sat high on his face. He was conventionally handsome. Handsome men have charisma. She'd seen it before. Charisma is dangerous. People trust it right away. It's alluring, charming, sweet.

Deadly.

Her dad had charisma. The landlord would come by about the rent money, and Dad would grin and say, "You know I'm good for it. How're the kids? That wife of yours still drivin' you nuts? Yeah, mine too. See you Friday at the bowl-o-rama. You'll have your money." And they would shake hands and pat each other on the back. It was charming, for sure, if you were on his side.

"I'm just going to grab a shower, then I'll start cooking," Al announced to the group. He turned to his wife and cradled her face in his hands. "Don't drink too much if you're going to go out tonight," he said in a high-pitched, sing-song tone.

Haisley pushed him away playfully. "Go shower," she said, matching his tone. When he left, Haisley topped off her drink.

"You okay?" Olivia asked.

"I'm great," Haisley said cheerfully. "Don't mind my husband."

Olivia nodded. She took her drink and followed Haisley five steps to the living area. Haisley knelt on the carpet, and Olivia found a spot on the couch.

"Damn, Haisley," Jara said, giving her a side-eye. "You didn't tell us your husband was a supermodel."

"When you've been with a man for half your life," Haisley said, leaving the sentence hanging. Haisley's eyes went down to the floor and then came back up as if they were falling in a dream and jumped to catch themselves. "So, ladies," she continued, "shall we play a round of never-have-I-ever to get to know each other a little better? I know you know how this works."

"Wow, throwback. I'm in. I haven't played this since college," Jara said.

"It's not my favorite, but I'll play," Paige said.

"Can you give us a refresher?" Jara asked.

"Okay," Haisley said, "I'll say a statement that starts with 'Never have I ever,' and you think about it. It will be something that I've truly never done. If it's something you *have* done, you take a drink. It'll be fun."

"You good with this, Paige?" Jara asked.

Paige rolled her eyes, and Jara chuckled.

Haisley went first. "Never have I ever stolen anything worth more than five dollars."

Olivia looked around the circle. Paige took a sip, and everyone laughed.

"You don't have to tell the story, but you can if you want to."

"I'll pass," Paige smirked.

"Okay, your turn Jara."

"Never have I ever gotten a tattoo."

"*What?*" Haisley responded.

"I've never had anything I've felt strongly enough to ink on my skin," Jara responded. "I've had so many friends over the years tell stories and post pictures of all kinds of tattoos, but they're just not my thing."

Olivia thought about the phases of the moon printed on Adira's upper arm. She imagined herself running a finger down them, circling each one. She blinked and shook her head, coming back to the moment.

Haisley and Paige put cups to their mouths and showed the various ink marks. A shamrock peeked from Haisley's sock. A lion roared from Paige's shoulder.

"I'm a Leo, baby, gotta have a lion," Paige said, relaxing into the game.

Al came into the room. "You're playing that game again?"

Haisley flashed him a tight smile. "Ignore my husband," she said to the women.

"Dinner will be ready soon," Al said. "You're all going to need something to sop up the alcohol."

Haisley rolled her eyes. "I was just kidding, honey. You know I love this game."

Al nodded, but his face stayed tense.

Olivia's throat itched with worry. Were they just teasing each other, or was something else going on between them?

Haisley turned to Paige. "Go ahead, Paige."

"Never have I ever," Paige started, plucking at one of her curls. Olivia was just waiting for her to say something about nepotism. Or getting a handout. Or riding on the coattails of a family member. "Never have I ever," Paige said again, "drank so much I had to throw up."

"Dang, girl. Did you go to college?" Jara asked, taking a sip. Haisley took one too.

Olivia gulped a tangy sip. A mint fragment wedged itself between two teeth, and she moved it out with her tongue. On her twenty-first birthday, Gina convinced her that long island iced tea would be the best way to start the celebration. Before dinner, her face hung over the toilet. *Maybe Al has a point.*

"Olivia, you go."

Olivia looked around at the women. She thought about things she had never done. *Never got a B. Never got a tattoo. Never got pulled over. Never been with a man. Never held back saying one of those things in order to be cool.* Well, that last one was a lie.

She adjusted the straps of her top. "Never have I ever been on a reality TV show."

All eyes turned to Jara as she took a long sip.

"Touché," Jara said. "I see you, girl."

Something warm fluttered within Olivia beyond the satisfaction stemming from competition. She pushed it away. *Stay focused.*

"Okay, I got one," Jara said. "Never have I ever done drugs."

The women exchanged glances. All of them kept their drinks in their laps.

"Well, that's a first," Jara said. Everyone laughed.

"Dinner's ready," Al announced, bringing each of them a plate. Olivia's mouth watered at the smell of fried onions. It had been hours and several drinks since she last ate any real food. She took a piece of fried fish in her hand and took a bite, burning the tip of her tongue.

"Let's keep playing," Haisley said, licking her fingers.

"I'll take a turn," Al said. "Never have I ever cheated on my spouse or partner."

What did he mean? Did Haisley cheat?

The air in the room got hot. After several moments, Paige sighed dramatically and took a sip of her drink. The moment passed and the group erupted in a series of "Wows" and "Oops." Collective astonishment.

"*What?*" Jara hollered.

Olivia studied Haisley's face. The corners of her mouth tipped into the slightest frown. Her eyes, trained on Paige, glistened.

"No way!" Olivia added, feeling the need to say something.

Paige pulled at a bobbing curl. "It wasn't that big of a deal. It was my eighth-grade boyfriend. He was away with his family on vacation during the winter dance."

When they finished dinner Haisley said, "All right, ladies. How about a trip to the bars? There's a great one I've been dying to show you."

Olivia looked down at her empty cup. Her head was starting to get foggy, but she had to admit she was having fun.

"First Friday night. Let's do it!" Jara said.

"I'll call us a car," Haisley said.

They stacked up the dishes and stumbled out into the night.

It was this moment, later, when Olivia would look back, that she would wish she had stopped drinking.

CHAPTER 16

The car, their capsule-sized party bus, pulled up to the curb, and all four of them piled in.

Olivia, still laughing at Paige's impression of Brian kicking the stable door, crawled into the middle between Jara and Paige. She settled into the soft seat and let her legs fall naturally into theirs.

"Crow's Nest Way?" The driver confirmed.

"That's the one," Haisley responded. "We'll show these ladies a good time." She whooped, and the women cheered.

"All right, then," the driver said, turning up the volume of the music.

The car swept north, and Olivia let herself be enveloped in the beat of the music and the bass bumping beneath her feet.

Paige asked, "What do you think your aunt is looking for in a winner?"

Insecurity rose from beneath the surface of her skin. She squeezed her hands between her thighs. "To be honest, I barely know her." If she could put some distance between herself and Margaret, maybe Paige and the others would see that there was no fast pass to the victory circle. Her connection with Margaret was nothing more than two people who knew each other once, a long time ago, and not for very long. For Olivia to win, she would have to work just as hard as anyone else.

"What do you mean?" Paige asked.

Olivia couldn't read the tone of her voice. "Margaret married my mother's older brother, but my mom and Tim were never close. We saw them at a holiday or two, but after my brother died—" Olivia stopped. She didn't want to turn the mood sour. "I don't know her well, is all I'm trying to say." She didn't know if it was the alcohol or the topic, but something inside her shifted, saddened. She was acutely aware that everyone in the car with her was a stranger; she knew so little about them.

"Well," Jara tapped her chin, "I think she's probably looking for skills, creativity, a good work ethic... Maybe a little fierceness."

Olivia exhaled, grateful to Jara for answering Paige's question. She made eye contact with Jara and mouthed, "Thank you."

Jara smiled back.

"Yeah, that tracks," Paige said.

Dark buildings rose higher and higher as they drove. The driver weaved around something in the road, a shredded tire or a dead possum. The car swerved down an alley between tall buildings and stopped next to a dumpster.

"Here we are," the driver said.

Olivia's mouth went dry as she stepped out into the darkness.

"Where are we, H?" Jara asked. "This some horror movie shit."

"Follow me, ladies," Haisley responded. "We're going to Bar 17. No one knows about this place except for a few people. It just opened at the start of this year. And the inside is much nicer than it looks from the outside."

Olivia stumbled forward down the dark alley. A cat cried somewhere nearby. Olivia moved with the others toward the flickering light above a door in the wall. She steadied herself and recommitted to the plan.

Be cool.

Olivia followed the women inside. Behind the reception station, lights danced off the disco balls and mirrors along the wall of Bar 17. People raised glasses at high tables. Bodies rubbed against each other on the dance floor. Olivia watched, as if through a camera lens, each person a character, everyone distant.

Haisley spoke to the hostess.

"There's a table by the bar right over there," she pointed. "It's all yours."

"Let's go, ladies," Haisley said.

Olivia moved along with the others and took a seat on a high stool. She scanned the faces of the people around her. She was at that stage of tipsy where every face she looked at closely was someone who she used to know.

A waiter approached the table, and they ordered a round of shots and water. Olivia let each ounce of liquid courage drip down her throat. Her head thrummed. A freckled man loosened his tie and called the bartender toward him with the snap of his fingers. A young woman in heels that would be way too high for Olivia tottered toward the bar while straightening her dress.

"What was it like being on a reality show?" Olivia asked Jara, starting a conversation, a friendship.

"It was mostly awesome." She tapped her fingernails on the table. "I'm trying to think of something to compare it to that you would understand. Being out in the wilderness for the show was kind of like how I imagine it feels to be the last one on set, alone, after a long day of filming, hungry and tired, still working, knowing you have to get the job done."

"Sounds cool." She almost asked what it felt like to win the show, but she didn't. She didn't want to give Jara the chance to consider that she might win the job too.

"Watching the show later, it wasn't that great, though. It's like any TV show, scripted and manipulated to tell a story."

Olivia nodded. "Still, must have been a cool experience."

Jara nodded. "For sure. Let's go dance," Jara said, pulling Paige by the elbow.

"You go have fun. I need a couple more drinks first," Haisley said. Her eyes followed the waiter who weaved between tables.

"Maybe later," Olivia said, taking a long drink of water. Lemon bit at her tongue, and she pursed her lips, waking up to the moment. The lemon, the drink, the jewelry, the dresses, the music—all of it swirled around her. She was ready to go home, back to comfort. Her mind was getting hazy from the alcohol.

Olivia fingered the water dripping down the side of her glass. Along the wall next to the bar, a red "Exit" light hung high in the corner. She looked down at the table and then back to the sign to make sure it wasn't the alcohol playing tricks on her.

Strange, since there's no door there.

Staring at it, she saw four people, two men and two women, walk through the wall. How many mint juleps had she had?

She leaned forward.

"You're trying to figure out that exit, huh?" Haisley said.

"I definitely saw some people go through that wall." Olivia scratched her chin. She fixed her eyes on the spot.

A group of people approached the door. Olivia studied their movements. A hand went to the brick, and a door in the wall opened. Light bounced off a man's bald head. Fizz. Olivia looked at the two people by his sides. Brian. Tiffany. They went through the door.

A spark of excitement fired in Olivia's chest.

Maybe I can talk to Brian.

"The door leads to a stairwell. There's a bar and lounge downstairs," Haisley said.

Olivia swallowed. If she could get a few minutes with Brian, she might be able to lay a strong foundation for their work together on set. She cleared her throat and said, "Can we go check it out?"

"Hell yes," Haisley said. "I'll show you. But when we go down there, let's find a spot away from Fizz. I've spent too much time with him this week."

Haisley looped her arm through Olivia's and led her to the wall across the room. Olivia ran her fingers over the bricks.

"Press the brick with the faint black outline," Haisley said.

Olivia did as she was told and pressed the brick. The door opened to a small landing and a staircase.

As they descended, the staircase became a muffled pathway. The music faded, and the noise stilled.

At the bottom of the flight of stairs, Olivia glanced around the lounge. On the left side of the room, people drank at the bar. The glow of stained-glass light emanated from liquor bottles. Around them, intimate groups clustered together in a variety of lounge areas.

In the dim light of the basement bar, Olivia searched for Brian.

She spotted him on a swanky leather couch near the end of the bar under a pool of orange light. Brian. Tiffany. Fizz. A couple of the extras.

"There are some seats at the end of the bar," Olivia said to Haisley, leading her forward. She made her way closer to Brian, putting herself in earshot.

At the bar, Haisley ordered another round. Olivia had no intention of drinking more. She strained to hear the conversation between Brian and the others. The words were muffled by laughter.

Olivia turned to face Haisley, who chatted with a bartender. Haisley's cheeks, flushed as red as the strawberry daiquiri in front of her, leaned forward and said, "You, my guy, make an excellent drink."

Olivia shook her head, but she was glad to see Haisley having a good time. She put the straw to her lips but didn't drink. Her head buzzed with alcohol and questions about how to connect with Brian.

What does a person say when they're trying to make friends with actors? "Hey"? "What's up"? "Great job this week"?

They were regular people—beautiful, talented, regular people.

Olivia imagined her conversation with Brian. "*You'll help me?*" He would ask, needing her. "*Of course, buddy, of course. I have just the thing.*" She pictured herself sitting knee-to-knee with Brian in the field behind the stables prodding the feelings out of him like a therapist. Their relationship had to start somewhere. Just a basic rapport. That was all she needed.

She took a series of deep breaths and peered, eyes round, at the other people in the basement bar. A few men around Noah's age, forties and fifties, sat quietly at the bar, drinks loosely cradled between their hands.

Olivia stood and moved toward the actors. Light glowed from artificial candles on a coffee table. Cologne and coconut rum commingled in the air.

"Hey, everyone," Olivia said, squeezing the cool drink in her hand.

The actors and some of the crew members continued merrily without paying attention to her. Her face burned. She turned away, but stopped when she heard, "Hey you're one of the fellows—Olivia, right?" Tiffany spoke from her spot on the couch. "Come join us."

"Great job this week," Olivia said, sitting in an open chair next to the couch where Brian and Tiffany sat. Fizz drank in a chair on the other end of the couch.

"Thanks," Tiffany said.

Brian fingered the last ice cube that had stuck to the bottom of the cup and poured it into his mouth. "Next week will be better," he said.

This was her chance. Olivia only needed a minute. "I have some ideas for how you can connect with your emotions in the upcoming scenes," she said to Brian. "I can help you."

Brian stared straight ahead. He didn't respond.

"Brian? I can help," she said louder. Through the foggy, alcohol-induced haze, she thought she saw him smile. Everything was going to work out.

But then he said, "What makes you think I need your help? Who are you, anyway? An intern?"

Fizz laughed and threw back another sip. "Don't be rude, Brian," he said sarcastically with a mouth full of beer. "The equity initiative that Margaret has going on won't last long anyway." Fizz spoke in a slurred, jolly manner.

Olivia swallowed. Words scrambled in her mind.

Say something. Anything. Apologize. Start again. This is going to ruin your life.

She felt Tiffany's eyes on her.

"Get us another round, Tiffany," Brian said, tapping her on the thigh. He snapped his head back against the top of the couch. "I need a drink."

Olivia stood up, tears welling at the back of her eyes. She retreated to the bar where Haisley and the bartender, faces only inches apart, played a game of tic-tac-toe on a napkin.

She took a deep breath and a long suck of the drink. She closed her eyes, and the whole world spun. Acid shot from her stomach to her mouth like flames up a pine tree; it was definitely time to go home.

I'll have to find another way to get through to him. She blinked her eyes open. *Or another way to win.*

CHAPTER 17

"I never need to drink that much again," Jara texted the group on Monday morning.

Same. Olivia had spent the rest of the weekend tending to her hangover.

She drove the golf cart down the street in the pre-dawn darkness. Her routines as the location manager had moved to muscle memory. The dark apartment building parking lot with flickering streetlights. Dense trees swaying, giant monsters. The clearing at the gates.

She entered the code at the gate, buzzing herself in, and parked the cart. She yawned. *Ten minutes from coffee.*

Before getting out of the cart, she opened her phone to the group text thread. Her thumbs lingered over the keys.

What to say back? She could keep it simple and go with "Same." She could give more detail: "Still thirsty. Head spinning." She wrote and revised messages in her head but didn't land on anything.

She stepped out of the cart and started down the path toward the house.

Maybe I'll let Haisley respond first.

She tripped as she closed her phone, catching herself palms down in the dirt. The phone fell to the ground. She wiped off her hands.

"What the—"

She lunged for her cellphone and clicked on its light to get a better look. She leaned against a forest green tarp in the path and pushed herself up. A rotting stench made her gag.

Her heart quickened.

"Holy shit," she said into the darkness.

She held her breath and lifted the corner of the tarp, hoping to see a piece of film equipment left haphazardly by some careless crew member.

Instead, she saw a face, loose flesh hanging from bones, hair pressed like string to the place above the forehead. Something wet like drool that had once seeped from between living lips pooled in the place where the chin should have been.

Two days before, Olivia had seen her alive, laughing in the glow of the basement bar. Now she was here. Rigid. Dead.

Tiffany.

Olivia steadied the phone in her hand and dialed 911. Inside, it felt as a can full of coins was being shaken in her stomach, the top of the can slamming into her ribs. Outside, she was still.

"Nine-one-one, what's your emergency?"

"Hi, this is Olivia Gabriel; I'm part of the team working on the TV show at Jasper Equestrian. I got here this morning and found one of the actresses lying on the ground under a tarp. I'm pretty sure she's dead."

The words came out even, smooth. Olivia wasn't surprised; she was good at handling crises. Most of the practice had come from classroom situations and around the school. Bee stings. Fights. A seizure. Active shooter drills.

Lice outbreaks. Even without the kid-witnesses obligating calmness, she knew how to do it.

"What's your address?"

"Fifty Jasper Way."

"We'll send someone over right away."

Olivia hung up the phone and then dialed again. "Margaret, it's Olivia. I've found Tiffany. She's dead." She spoke quickly and steadily, wanting to make sure she was understood.

"Olivia, slow down. What are you talking about?" Margaret's voice was clear and calm.

"I'm here on set, and I found Tiffany lying under a tarp in the parking area." Olivia took a deep breath, trying to hold down the creeping panic. "There's drool on her face. She's not moving."

"Is anyone else with you? I'll call nine-one-one."

"No, it's just me. I already called." Olivia's heart raced. On the ground, Tiffany's body lay stiff.

"Hang tight. I'll be right there."

Olivia's breath came out in huffs. She needed to get away from there, away from Tiffany. *The body.* Away from the stench that was steadily imprinting itself on her memory.

She used the cellphone light to guide her toward the safety of the stables. She reached her arm toward the inside wall and flipped on the light. The place was empty again, the property owners and their horses having come and gone over the weekend.

In the stillness, Olivia caught her breath. The last moment she saw Tiffany was when she left the basement bar on Friday night. *Wasn't it?*

Her memory hazed over like a tossed Etch A Sketch.

Blue lights bounced off the gates. The police car approached, and Olivia moved toward it. The wind blew, and a piece of sand burned her eyes. She rubbed them as she hurried to the gate to let the officer through.

The main entrance to Jasper Equestrian was the gate. The only way through the gate was the keypad if you knew the code, the buzzer from the office, and the buzzer on the inside of the gate itself. *The only people who know the code are me, Margaret, and Noah.* She scratched her chin, nicking off a piece of skin.

Aside from the gate, the place was surrounded by fence on three sides and water on the other. Unless Tiffany had arrived by boat, she would have needed the passcode to enter.

Olivia opened the gate and directed the officer to the spot behind the stables. She left the gate open so everyone else could get through.

The officer parked and got out of the car. His name, Mitchell, was etched on his silver name badge. He raised a flashlight and strode past Olivia. He lifted the tarp and leaned over Tiffany's face, looking at her like an unwanted pizza topping.

"I think she's dead," Olivia said. "She was here like this when I pulled in this morning. I fell on her." Olivia's phone shook in her hands. She turned off the light and slid the phone into her pocket.

"We'll let the crime scene folks handle that," he said, standing straight again and poking the tarp nonchalantly with the toe of his boot. "Medical examiner should be here soon."

When the van pulled up, the medical examiner went to Tiffany, and a woman in a uniform approached Olivia.

"Are you hurt?" the uniformed woman asked.

"No, I'm fine," Olivia said.

"We're going to take a quick look at you. That okay?"

Olivia nodded.

When she was done, the uniformed woman said, "You should clear out of the area, but don't go too far. The police are going to need to ask you some questions. You have somewhere to wait?"

"Yeah, I can go inside, but a lot of people are on their way here." Olivia checked the time on her phone. People would start arriving soon, and it was her week for filming.

My week. It's my week. Her stomach tangled into a tight knot.

"Let them know you're closed for today. This is a crime scene."

Olivia nodded. "Of course." She wrapped her knuckles on her forehead. *Of course.*

Waves of jumbled emotions coursed through her body. She swallowed as she watched Margaret's car approach.

Margaret drove through the gate and parked her fancy car. She checked her lipstick and teeth in the rearview mirror.

Olivia paced back and forth in the dirt.

Margaret stepped out of the car and adjusted her pants around her knees. She strode leisurely toward Olivia. "Are you all right?" She folded Olivia into an awkward hug.

Margaret was saying the right words, making the right moves, but it felt scripted. Olivia let her fingers rest along Margaret's bony back for a moment. The starchy shirt made Olivia's face itch. "I'm okay," Olivia lied, pulling away. The wind, dry and grainy, struck her lips.

"What happened?" Margaret asked.

She shrugged, and then it hit her. Margaret wanted to know what happened because Olivia should *know* what happened. She was the location manager. She oversaw the safety and security of all members of the cast and crew. Her cheeks flushed hot. "I can check the cameras."

"Good girl," Margaret said. "But what happened to Tiffany?"

Olivia heard Margaret's question, but she felt dazed, out of it, like she was there but not there at the same time. "She's dead," Olivia said.

Margaret's hand prickled at Olivia's back. "Go into the office, Olivia. Sit down a minute. Maybe get some coffee. I'm going to talk to the officer, and then I'll come find you."

Olivia hurried into the office and woke the sleeping computer. She opened the files as Noah had shown her how to do. *Maybe I should start back with Friday when we left the set. Friday.* "Fuck," she said. On Friday she had been the last to leave, and she wasn't a hundred percent sure she had closed the gate. *Had it clicked?* She couldn't remember hearing the sound.

For a split second, she entertained a crazy thought. *I could delete that video. No one would ever know.* She shook her head. *This is a crime scene.*

She held her hand on the mouse but didn't move the cursor. *Maybe the police should be doing all of this.* But curiosity took control of her hand, and she clicked the file for Friday night.

Her mouth fell open. *What the...*

She clicked back to the main folder and opened Saturday. Then Sunday. She gasped.

Nothing.

The folders were empty.

Olivia stood and backed away from the computer. Fear glued her feet to the ground.

The door opened, and Margaret walked in. "How are you holding up?" Margaret asked.

A test. Olivia swallowed. "I'm doing okay, given the circumstances." She stood taller, straightening herself. "What can I do to help?"

Margaret sighed. "Well, the police are taking care of the next steps. This is such a tragedy." Margaret's head shook back and forth. "I'm not sure what this will mean for us, but I need to let people know what happened. I'm going to send out a message to the team."

Heat rose on Olivia's arms and face. A strange sensation passed through her. *On Friday, Tiffany was alive, and today, she's dead.* Olivia rubbed at her chest. The walls closed in around her. She needed to get some air, but she didn't move.

Olivia thought about the people who would call Tiffany's family. How would they break the news? How does one comfort someone who loses a family member?

Olivia sunk back into the chair and cupped her shoulder, feeling the soft, thin skin. The events of that morning warped her back to 1997. It was winter. Several inches of snow had fallen during the funeral.

A ten-year-old version of herself lay on the floor in the darkness outside her mom's bedroom. The carpet scratched her chin, but she didn't move. The burnt smell of overcooked lasagna lingered in the hallway. Long cries seeped from behind the bedroom door.

The slam of the front door an hour before reverberated through the house. Her dad stared coldly at her mother, speaking his final, stinging words: "It's your fault he's dead." The words still echoed in her brain, hollowing out her heart. She wanted to go into the room, put an arm around her mom, and tell her it wasn't her fault Billy was dead. She wanted to tell her they would be all right. They had each other, and they would be okay. She missed her brother too.

But she didn't know how her mom would react, so she stayed on the floor. She pressed a hand over her mouth to stifle the cries that threatened to spring out of her like the ear-splitting screams of a puma. She squeezed her cold toes into the backs of her knees. She closed her eyes and fell asleep, numb.

Tiffany's family shouldn't have to suffer.

"We're so sorry for your loss," someone would say to Tiffany's parents.

What would it be like to lose a child? The grief would be intolerable. Something loosened within her. All those years ago her sadness for her mom had turned to anger when she grew into a teenager, and the distance between them never closed. A tear welled in the corner of an eye.

She was doing the best she could.

CHAPTER 18

Olivia emerged from the office in a daze. People milled about the house. Coffee mugs clinked on glass countertops. Murmurs swept down the hallways. The low buzz of people processing the news whirred like static.

Jara and Haisley huddled together in the living room at the front of the house. Paige sat nearby, as if absorbing comfort from the other two.

Haisley held a mug close to her lips with both hands. "Olivia, are you okay? Al said you were the first one here," she said quickly.

I was the first one here. Where had Noah been? "Yeah," Olivia managed to say.

"Fuck," Jara said.

The front door opened and closed as people moved in and out of the house.

Haisley asked, "Do you need anything? I'll go get you some coffee." She fled toward the kitchen.

"Can we still be here?" Olivia asked.

"Police say just not in the yellow tape." Jara shrugged. "It's probably easier for them if we're here if they need to ask us any questions."

Outside the front window, uniformed people moved in and out of the marked area.

Olivia, lightheaded, staggered forward and took a seat on the upholstered chair next to Paige.

"You okay?" Jara asked.

Olivia nodded. Her head spun, and her whole body felt weak, heavy.

Haisley returned with coffee and a pack of peanut butter crackers. "You should eat something," Haisley suggested.

Olivia opened the package and bit into a cracker.

"What do you think happened to her?" Paige asked.

Olivia shook her head. Paige's question unlocked a series of new questions. How did she die? Did someone hurt her? How did she get here? Why didn't the property owners find her this weekend?

The door opened, and Noah and Margaret walked through. Margaret had a phone pressed to her ear. "No, I don't care who it is, just send us someone who looks like her." They stormed through the living room and down the hallway. Already problem-solving.

"She was so nice," Haisley said.

"Seriously," Jara added.

"What's going to happen to the show?" Paige asked.

They all shrugged. Olivia brushed cracker crumbs from her lips and went back into the package for another when she smelled a familiar vanilla. She looked up.

"Just wanted to see how you're doing," Adira said, kneeling next to Olivia. "Do you need anything?"

Olivia wiped the corners of her mouth with her thumb and forefinger to dust off cracker remnants. "I'm all set. Thank you for checking," she said, keeping eye contact with Adira as if to say, "What I really need is a hug."

Adira's eyes, warm and soft, lingered on Olivia's as if to say, "I'll find you later when there aren't as many people around." But what came out of her mouth was, "Everything has been set up out front, but let me know if there's anything else." With a smile, Adira went back outside.

Olivia looked at the faces of the other women to see if they understood the conversation beneath the conversation, but they all still had the worried eyes of people who were a hundred feet away from a dead person.

The answers to the questions weren't in the living room.

"I'm going to go check in with Noah," Olivia said.

The women nodded, and Olivia weaved back down the hallway to the office. Her body didn't feel right, but she pushed down the discomfort so that she could focus.

"They'll want to interview you," Noah said as Olivia walked through the office door.

Olivia nodded.

"You okay?"

She nodded again. How was she supposed to describe the torrent inside her? "Strange that she's dead," Olivia said.

"I know. What a shame," Noah went back to typing on the computer.

Olivia plopped into the chair behind him.

Noah looked up. "I hope you don't do drugs," he said like a lazy father, thinking it might be important to check but not wanting to have the conversation.

"Drugs?"

"Oh, I'm just assuming, based on her history." He shifted his weight in the chair. "We'll know for sure after the autopsy. You never know." He shrugged. His light-blue eyes were bloodshot. A million tiny veins prickled away from his pupil.

Her mind went to her brother's baby cheeks and the prickly softness of his summer buzzcut. To the teacher's dumb reaction at the funeral. Shoulders pressed tightly toward his ears. A stupid "what more could we have done" smirk.

Bile burned in Olivia's esophagus. Anger fired in her chest like heat in a kiln. She felt an intense need to protect Tiffany as she had felt for her brother. They weren't alive to defend themselves.

"Why weren't you here this morning?" she asked. If Noah had been there, he would have been the one to discover Tiffany. She ran a finger along the scratches, still burning, on her palms.

"I slept at the hotel last night. You doing okay, Sherlock? It must have been shocking for you to be the first one here."

Olivia nodded. "I just thought you would be here. You're always here first." She held her breath, startled at the words coming out of her mouth.

Noah spoke cheerfully like the whole situation was no big deal to him. "What I do outside of work isn't exactly your business. But if you must know, I was with my lover last night."

The way he said the word "lover" made Olivia's skin prickle. She didn't know what else to say.

"What about the property owners? Where were they?"

"Property owners didn't come back this weekend. Horse competition. Remember?"

Olivia shook her head. With all the prep she had been doing to get ready for her week as first assistant director, she must have missed that detail.

"Is everything ready for the shoot today?" Noah asked, changing the topic.

"Cops said we were off today."

"No, we're on. We're moving everything to the stables and the yard in the back. Of course, we might have people going in and out, and you will need to go into the police station at some point, but we're filming. Set up for the first scene, kiddo. This is your week."

Olivia searched his face for signs of sarcasm, but there were none. "You're serious?"

"As a heart attack."

Too soon.

"We'll let them do their jobs, and we'll do ours. The show goes on." He walked down the hallway.

Olivia shook her arms and legs, hoping the movement would expel the fog from her head. She took a deep breath, got her iPad out of her backpack, and headed for the stables.

Outside, heavy air clogged her lungs. She walked quickly to the stables, tied her hair up and out of her face as she walked, and yanked the door open. Light poured in through the opening at the other side. Manure composted in her nostrils.

Brian paced in front of the third horse stall, alone, holding a script in one hand and a shovel in the other. She stopped dead. Embarrassment crept up her face. She hadn't seen him since the basement bar. *Friday night.* When she was drunk, trying to connect with him seemed like an Academy Award worthy idea. She ducked into the first stall and gently raked the coarse hay, trying not to scrape the rake on the ground

From his spot in front of the stall two doors away, she heard him practicing, "I'm sorry, Momma. This is what I have to do. I don't want to do it, but you've given me no choice."

Bang! The shovel came crashing down on a metal stool used by the horse trainers. Again and again, Brian practiced the lines and then *whack*! She couldn't deny it; he was getting better.

She shook out the maroon horse blanket and replaced it over the door of the horse stall.

Brian repeated his lines. *How was he feeling about Tiffany's death?* For some people, throwing themselves into work and not thinking about the bad things happening around them was the best way forward. *Maybe I should do that too.*

Stepping back, she looked at the stall. Based on the shot list, using a second camera might be a good idea. A handheld one, maybe, angled from underneath the stool, could give an interesting perspective to the murder of Brian's character's mother. As part of the evaluation, Olivia would get feedback on her set work. Margaret and the others would see what she could do with a camera. She made a mental note to use a wide-angle shot for the first few seconds of the murder scene. *Murder scene.* Her mouth watered, a sign that vomit might follow.

The door opened, and Al and Margaret walked toward her. Al crossed his arms and said, "We're going to need you to come down to the station and answer some questions. It's important that we get your statement while the details are fresh."

Margaret said, "I'll have JD and Jara there with me today, and you can start your turn as first AD when you get back."

Olivia couldn't hold back the bile rising toward her mouth. She ran out of the stable and leaned against the wall.

Lurching forward, she puked.

CHAPTER 19

In her thirty-two years of life, she had never seen the inside of a police station. She never interacted much with the police, aside from an occasional situation or two, when an officer had come to the school for reasons unknown to her. The sight of police officers rattled something inside her, making her feel like a kid, guilty for no reason.

Al led her past a row of officers typing behind computers. She shrank into herself and steadied her eyes on the tiled floor in front of her. A bleach-like smell, likely rising from the yellow bucket between the men's and women's bathrooms, overpowered her nostrils, but she didn't scratch her nose like she wanted to. Her arms stayed straight by her sides.

In a small, gray room, Al pointed to a chair. The steel bit into her thighs, and she adjusted her shorts to cover more of her skin. *I should have brought a sweatshirt.*

Al sat across from her, looking at her with deep brown eyes. "I'll be leading this investigation. Whatever you share in the interview will be used in the investigation, but no one will know you're the informant, if that's a concern. You can trust me. I want to get to the bottom of this." Al spoke steadily as if he'd done this a thousand times.

Olivia nodded.

"So, Olivia. Is it true you were the first person to arrive at Jasper Equestrian this morning?"

Olivia bit her lip and nodded.

"How did you find Tiff—" He hesitated. "How did you find the body?"

"I found her on the ground under a tarp. I tripped over her when I was walking."

"Did you see anything else?"

Olivia shook her head. She squeezed her trembling hands together.

"Based on what we found at the scene, Tiffany may have died from a drug overdose. Won't be sure until we get the results of the autopsy. Are you aware of anyone using drugs on set?" he asked.

Olivia slid her hands under her thighs. She thought back to her interaction with Tiffany at the bar. Tiffany smiled in the glowing light when she had said, "Hey, you're one of the fellows—Olivia, right? Come join us."

This doesn't make sense. She hadn't been drinking that much. Had she?

"No," she said. "I've never seen anyone use drugs."

"Did you know Tiffany personally?"

"Not really. I mean, I've seen her on the set. She usually arrives near the end of the group in the mornings, and she comes alone. Gets dropped off by one of the ride-sharing services."

"When was the last time you saw her?"

"I saw her on Friday night at the bar. Bar 17."

"Who did she hang around with?" he asked.

"Everyone, kind of. She was friendly. Didn't act in the way I'd expect for a person who uses drugs." Olivia's hands warmed, but a chill ran down her spine.

"Margaret Roark shared that, aside from Noah Sherman, you are the person who will see the most given your position. We'll do a thorough investigation, but we can't see everything, so we need you to keep your eyes peeled. Let us know if you see anything that looks off."

"No one else saw anything?" Olivia asked.

"Not yet—or not that we know of, anyway," he said. "Probably just a simple drug overdose."

She swallowed. *Troubled kid.* That's what they had said about her brother, Billy. *Should I mention the cameras?* Her mind tossed the idea back and forth. She had access to the cameras, so they might think she was the one to delete the videos. *Who else could have done that?* She bit the inside of her cheek. In truth, any one of them would have the ability to delete the files. *But why?* And what if the videos showed she had left the gate unlocked on Friday?

She would let the detectives do their jobs.

"We'll get to the bottom of this," Al said, standing from the chair and sliding a business card across the table. "Give me a call if you see anything. Be good out there, Olivia."

Outside in the heat, tears sprang from her eyes. She walked the four blocks back to the apartment. She needed some time to regroup before going back to set. Back inside, she laid down on the bed and cried.

When she closed her eyes, the memory of the stench of the body assaulted her nose, so she opened them again. She replayed the conversation with Al. She could still feel the nipping cold of the chair in the interrogation room. The questions he asked. The answers she gave.

I should have told him about the videos. She reached for the phone to call Al, and then she stopped. *What am I doing?*

She dropped the phone back onto the bed and rubbed her forehead. A tornado swirled inside her.

What am I doing here?

The cardinals stared at her from the windowsill. Her mind went to her grandfather. She was a child again. Sleeping in the darkness. Grandpa at the door. "Go to sleep," he whispered. "We'll talk again in the morning."

She wished she could go to sleep now and wake up in a year. She cradled the pillow between her arms and closed her eyes. There would be nothing more to worry about. No pressure from anyone. No one to impress. No confusion, loss, or grief.

Her body relaxed on the bed.

If I gave up, if I quit the competition, I would be free. At the thought, guilt immediately overtook her. What would Tiffany think if she could see her now? What would Billy think? She opened her eyes widely and bit the inside of her cheek. A few weeks before, she listened in the cafeteria to the announcement of the school closure. A get-out-of-school-free pass handed to her with the added bonus of securing an opportunity in film. She thought back to her students asking, "What are your goals, Ms. G?"

I can't let them down.

She flipped over the pillow and rested her cheek again on the cool side. She slowed her breathing. What would it be like back on set without Tiffany?

I should have known the signs.

These were the consequences, she told herself, for not paying enough attention.

She picked up her phone and scrolled through her list of contacts. She could call Brad, but what would she say? "Hey friend, miss you. Nothing new here except one of the actresses *died* on set, and I found her body. Now the police are questioning me. How are things going with *you*?"

Let's go, Olivia. This is your job. She could be a great location manager and maybe even a great director someday. She could tell the stories that needed to be told. Billy's. Tiffany's. Wake the world up and compel them into action. Get them to notice. Actors are conduits for these messages. Their portrayal of real-life emotions pulled at the heartstrings of the people who were still alive. Directors get the message across in the most compelling way possible.

And today is my day to direct, to lead.

To tell a story to an audience.

Get up.

She pulled herself up and stood by the bed. She lifted the cardinal painting from the windowsill and looked closely at her grandfather's signature in the corner. His memory calmed her. Her body remembered the feeling that she got when she sat with him, knowing that he wanted her to succeed. Warmth spread across her chest.

I'm going to do this, Grandpa. I can do this.

She grabbed her backpack and slid out of the apartment.

Outside, the flag for Monarch blew in the breeze. Craving the comfort of others, she turned and went into the coffeeshop. A few clusters of people sipped drinks at tables, but no one waited in line.

Olivia waved, and Adira came out from behind the counter. Olivia rushed forward and wrapped her arms around Adira, melting into her. Adira's fingers caressed the back of Olivia's head.

"It's going to be okay," Adira said softly.

Tears streamed down Olivia's face. She held Adira tightly, not wanting to let go.

CHAPTER 20

The set in and around the stables was like an army war camp without the tents. People walked around the caution tape. Set props littered the grass. Boxes of pizza were spread across the food table.

Olivia walked into the stables. Margaret and Jara huddled together over a tablet in the center alley between two rows of stalls.

Olivia approached them.

"You're back," Margaret said. "We're about to film the next scene."

"I'm good to keep going if she needs more time," Jara said to Margaret.

"I'm here. I'll take it," Olivia said. She smiled at Jara.

Jara frowned and stepped back.

"The new Tiffany will arrive tomorrow," Margaret said, "so we'll keep filming the scenes that she's not in."

The new Tiffany. Olivia fought another wave of nausea.

"Will she be ready?" Olivia asked.

Margaret nodded. "Better be."

Olivia pulled the tablet out of her bag and opened the call sheet. She checked the set arrangement to make sure everything was in place. *Focus.*

Haisley held half a bagel between her teeth in the second stall as she climbed a ladder. She leaned over into stall one and adjusted the lighting above Brian's head. Fizz stood close to her, nipping at her heels.

Paige tinkered with the camera outside the first stall, where the actors prepared for action. On the camera, a clear picture showed both actors, Brian and Maria. Olivia reviewed the notes and glanced at the preview on the camera. *Perfect.*

From the space behind her, she smelled coffee. She could feel Margaret breathing like a judge on a reality singing competition, critique at the ready. Olivia imagined that was how those singers felt going through the audition, wondering if the voice they'd been listening to as they sang in the shower all those years was *actually* good or only good inside their head.

Except here, Margaret, hands folded into her cargo shorts, leaned forward on her toes, ready to take the lead at any moment. A warm, snaking pressure squeezed Olivia's chest. She rubbed at her head, feeling an emerging headache pinching at her temples.

Her hand quivered as she scrolled through the notes. *Focus.*

The makeup artist dabbed Brian's face with a brush and ruffled his hair.

The actress, Maria, playing the role of Brian's elderly mom, took a sip of water from a flask. "If I wanted to be drinking, I'd be at the bar. This keeps the water cool, and I only need a sip," she said as if someone were judging her.

The sarcasm reminded Olivia of her mom, and at that moment, she missed her. But the *missing* was more like *longing.*

"Final checks, please," Olivia called, assuming the role of the first assistant director.

"Louder," Margaret said to Olivia without expression. Her neutral tone gave no hint of what she was thinking.

"Final checks, please!"

Brian and Maria took their spots in the stall, becoming Gregory Sky and Momma.

"Quiet on the set!" The words shook coming out of Olivia's mouth.

Maria sat on one of two stools, ready to soak hay in a bucket. Brian reached into the pocket of his overalls and pulled out a pair of glasses. Olivia checked her notes.

He's not supposed to be wearing glasses in this scene.

She froze, not knowing whether she should tell him or let him run with it. *A creative choice?* He seemed focused, so she held her breath and called, "Action!"

Gregory Sky sprang to life. His eyes were laser beams pointed down at Momma.

"Why'd you have to tell the police, Momma?" he asked, leaning over the bony woman.

"I care about you, son. I want you to get help," she whimpered.

"I'm sorry, Momma. This is what I have to do. I don't want to do it, but you've given me no choice." He brought the shovel up over his head.

"*Cut!*" Margaret called from the other side of the camera.

Margaret pulled the actors and Olivia together in a huddle. Olivia's internal temperature felt like it had raised several degrees from embarrassment. The scene had been going well.

Hadn't it?

Margaret turned to face Brian. "I'm not sure those glasses work for this scene. Though I have to say the lines came out fantastic. And the emotion was perfect. We could feel Gregory's anger at the betrayal of his mother."

"I have to wear the glasses," Brian said.

Margaret's face twisted in thought. "What do you think, Olivia?"

Olivia put her hand to her chin. She addressed Brian, "The glasses work well for your nice guy scenes. Since this is the one where the audience will see your chaotic side, I think it will be better to see the intensity of your eyes if you do this one without the glasses."

She held her breath while she waited for his response. Compliments had worked with Brian in the past.

Brian's eyes were lasers.

The hair on her arms stood as straight as spikes.

"I'll try it. But if it doesn't go well, the glasses are coming back." He went back to his place in the stall.

Margaret half-smiled, which was enough for Olivia to know she had done a fine job. Some of the chats between takes had ended with Brian wandering around the set with his head down, mumbling for several minutes. The fact that he had agreed to do another take was good. His agreement to go without the glasses was a bonus. Olivia exhaled.

"Quiet on the set!"

The air was still, as if all crew members had sucked in all they would need for the next two minutes.

"Action!"

"Why'd you do it, Momma?" he asked.

"Oh baby, I'm only trying to help," Momma pleaded. Fake tears seeped through her eye makeup.

"I'm sorry, Momma. This is how it's going to go. I don't want to do it, but you've given me no choice." He cocked the shovel up over his head, and this time, he released it hard against the second metal stool, two feet from Maria.

The scene ended.

"That was great!" Margaret said. "Awesome, awesome!"

Olivia smiled at Brian. His eyes were fixed on the end of the shovel that he was still gripping in his hand.

"We'll have Paige play that back to ensure we have what we need. Otherwise, we'll be good to go."

Paige brought the camera over to them, and Olivia and Margaret leaned toward the small screen to watch the playback.

The acting was terrific, but the lighting was off.

"We fucked up," Paige said. "Haisley must have lowered the light between takes."

Olivia's heart sank. There was a halo of light around Brian's head.

"You told me to lower it," Haisley said to Fizz.

"No, I didn't," Fizz argued.

Haisley and Fizz locked eyes.

Olivia held her elbows as Margaret walked into the stall to talk to the actors.

Margaret said, "Listen, guys, we have to do one more take. The lighting was off. Do it exactly the same as before."

"Are those amateurs going to get it right this time, for fuck's sake?" Brian asked.

Olivia and Haisley exchanged glances. *Murder in Morristown* was Brian's first big show. He was more of an amateur than some of the fellows.

"One more time, and we've got it," Margaret said. Margaret backed out of the stall toward the camera, giving Brian a thumb's up like she was handing a lollipop to a good little boy sitting still for half a second at a doctor's office.

Brian performed the scene again without any issues. Olivia breathed a sigh of relief.

"That's a wrap," Margaret called.

The crew began to pack up. Olivia lingered by Margaret.

"Excellent job," Margaret said.

The air around Olivia lightened. "Thank you."

"You did well. It's not easy to cajole actors, and it's a big part of this job. If you keep working at it, there's a chance you'll be ready for an assistant director role."

Olivia grinned, brushing wisps of hair off her cheek. She was nine years old again, basking in the warm glow of a rare smile from her mom.

I need to keep doing well.

Olivia closed her tablet and opened her handheld camera, catching a shot of the dispersal of actors and crew. Through the lens, she captured Brian, who stayed behind to practice. He had his moments, but he was one of the hardest-working people on set.

She capped the camera and went over to Brian. "How are you doing?"

"Good enough," he said.

"I'd love to help if there's a part of a scene that you're not feeling good about." Olivia looked away and then back. "Any part of the upcoming scenes you want to talk through?" The words stumbled out of her mouth. She thought about rephrasing but instead waited.

He stared at her. She couldn't read the expression on his face. "I appreciate your enthusiasm. Acting is a beautiful thing. I wish my family could see that."

She didn't know how to respond. She wondered about Brian's family, whether he had lost them or had one of those families that everyone else seemed to have. The together kind. Maybe something in between.

When Olivia lost her family, she lost them all at once, and from that night, a void spread within her. The hole wasn't like a missing jigsaw puzzle piece. It was like a chunk of her heart had been cut out. The blood had to find a new way to pump. Over time she adapted, but the stuff inside her still felt different, off.

"How are you doing about Tiffany?" she asked.

"I'd rather not talk about it," he said gruffly, lowering his head.

She retreated. Succeeding with him required a balance between giving him space and finding the right words to motivate him. She uncapped the camera and panned to catch a shot of the empty stables when she felt a hand on her back.

CHAPTER 21

Olivia jumped, and Adira's hand dropped like a lazy autumn leaf from Olivia's shoulder.

"I didn't mean to scare you. Noah said some people would be working late tonight, so I'm dropping off some food for dinner. I thought I'd come to check on you," Adira said, brushing a strand of hair behind her ear. Deep calm emanated from her smile.

Like water to the lips of a desert nomad, in Adira's presence, Olivia began to taste something she hadn't had in a while. Desire.

Olivia smiled. "I'm okay," she said. Residual shock came and went. She zipped the camera bag closed. With the day's filming over, the office work would start again. She tucked the tablet into her backpack.

"I need to go unload the van, but I also wanted to ask you about the catering orders," Adira said. The words came out in slow wisps, but they hit Olivia like a tsunami.

She deflated and panicked all at once like a popped balloon. *Monday. The catering orders.* In the haste of preparation for the scenes and the morning's events, she had forgotten to submit them.

"It's okay. I used last week's orders for today—no big deal. Let's get some dinner, and we can meet in the office.

We'll do them together," Adira smiled and ran a hand down Olivia's arm. "It will be okay."

Olivia hesitated and then nodded. What else had she forgotten to do? *The gate.* The muddled memory haunted her.

Olivia walked with Adira out to the catering van. Adira unloaded trays and lined them in a row on the table. To make herself useful, Olivia set out the hand-written food labels next to each tray while Adira fired the warmers beneath. Smells of pasta mingled with lavender.

Members of the cast and crew began to cluster around the table.

Adira came by and brushed a strand of hair off Olivia's face and tucked it behind Olivia's ear. She said, "I'll be two more minutes. Just need to make sure everyone is good to go."

Adira walked away, and Olivia heard a familiar voice behind her. "*Ooooohh,*" a high-pitched voice rang. "I'm a fan of this!" Haisley said, moving her pointer finger back and forth quickly between Olivia and Adira. "She's like the nicest person ever. You two would be so cute."

Olivia's face warmed, but she smiled at Haisley. "I don't know what you're talking about," she said playfully. Olivia chose a paper plate from the top of the stack, and Haisley followed in the buffet line behind her.

From the van, Adira called, "Anyone with dietary restrictions, make sure to check the labels."

"And she's thoughtful too. Always has been," Haisley said as if Olivia hadn't noticed.

Olivia smiled and added a dinner roll to her plate.

Adira closed the doors of the van. "Let's do this."

Inside, the office air conditioner whirred sweetly. Sweat cooled on Olivia's skin as she stacked papers into a neat pile to make room for their plates on the small square table. One folding chair for each of them. They sat down, and Olivia pulled out her tablet to open the spreadsheet.

"You can access it okay?" Adira asked.

Olivia nodded, suddenly aware that this was the most *alone* they had been with one another. The words "first date" came to mind, but she pushed them away, hoping to avoid the pressure that came with them.

On the spreadsheet, Olivia opened to the current week's tab. She copied over the orders from the previous week. "I'm basically copying and pasting. Is that right?"

"You can do that, but people might like some variety. Pull another option from the main list for one or two of the meals at least," Adira suggested.

Olivia nodded as Adira pinched two pieces of ziti together on her fork and put them between her lips. Even when she ate, Adira was unhurried, patient.

Olivia finished the orders and said, "Thank you for doing this with me."

Adira smiled. "I'm happy to help, but you know, I'm not just here for the orders."

Olivia raised an eyebrow.

"Tell me about you. What do you do when you're not working here?" Adira asked.

Olivia thought about the question. "Well, prior to this I was a teacher. My whole life was school," she said. When the words came out, she realized they weren't hers. They were Gina's words in Olivia's voice. She wiped the corner of her mouth with a napkin, drank a sip of water, and cleared her throat. "I really love film and storytelling.

When I'm not here, I'm working on projects of my own or watching movies. I used to spend a lot of time teaching, which I loved, but my school closed suddenly, and this opportunity came up. I also love coffee, long walks on the beach… Just kidding. Well, not kidding about coffee. I do love that."

Adira laughed. "Very cool. Me too. About coffee, of course."

A smile spread across Olivia's face. "How about you?" she asked. "What do you do when you're not setting out food and serving coffee?"

Adira shrugged. "I do ceramics. I like other things too… I like to swim and watch TV. But I spend most of my time in a shed outside my house making pots. Maybe you can come over sometime, and I'll show you."

Olivia examined the flecks on Adira's shirt. *Clay.* "That would be awesome," she said. In between bites of pasta and sips of water, Olivia began to feel the butterflies take flight and an ease spread through her like she was relaxing into a luxurious couch. There was a tenderness to Adira's voice, a gentleness in the way she moved. If Olivia inhaled deeply enough, she thought she might taste honey.

When she took the last sip of water, her tongue sprung loose. A dose of confidence, squeezed like juice from a Fruit Gusher, came from some unknown place within Olivia, and she said, "I'd love to see your art. We have nothing scheduled here on Saturday. Are you free then?"

"I have to work in the morning, but I'm free in the afternoon. How's two o'clock?" Adira smiled.

"That's perfect. I can't wait to see your creations."

"It's a date then," Adira said.

Electricity coursed through Olivia.

There was a knock at the door, and Margaret appeared. "I'm heading out for the night. I'll see you in the morning."

"Sounds good," Olivia said. Her mind ticked through her to-do list. She opened the tablet to the call sheet for the next day.

"Duty calls?" Adira asked.

"I dream of being her someday." Olivia gestured toward the door.

"I hope you keep your kindness when you take on that role," Adira said, smiling. She stood and moved toward the door. "I'll let you get to it. See you tomorrow."

Keep my kindness. What did that mean? Margaret's focus stayed on the show and filming. Those were the things that mattered to her. Olivia packed the tablet into her backpack, preparing to finish prep at home. Could a person have both? A career *and* relationships?

The familiar queasy moisture gathered in Olivia's mouth. Being with Adira washed away the images of death from her mind. But, when Olivia was alone, they all came rushing back.

CHAPTER 22

"What the hell?" Brian said in a matter-of-fact voice from his spot in the stables. He looked up and then back down at his phone. He scratched at the scruffy brown goatee he had grown as part of his costume.

It was Friday, and everything had been going smoothly. The images from Monday morning gradually faded from a constant background in Olivia's mind; they were still there but dulled. She had slept for four hours, which, she thought, was the most sleep she'd had in a night since moving to Jasper Cliffs.

Brian charged out of the stall, white T-shirt flapping under the industrial-sized fans, and approached Margaret. "The show is going to be canceled? What the fuck am I going to do?" Brian wailed.

The air smelled of horse shit and flies. Olivia's heart began to beat faster. What was Brian talking about?

Moments before, Olivia scanned the stables to make sure everything was in place. Lights? Good. Haisley took care of them. Cameras? Paige was there working on them. The script that Jara edited was looking good. Interesting. Margaret hung back with a notebook and pen, assessing. Even Noah joined to see her final performance of the week.

Given that it was her last chance to show her skills, Olivia double-checked everything. Lights. Cameras. Script.

Brian's meltdown thwarted her plans.

She opened a browser on her tablet and searched the headlines. She read, "Lead actor on a TV show being filmed in Jasper Cliffs unpopular with fans."

Fizz came out from behind the lights. "We're not being canceled. Right, Margaret?"

Margaret addressed the group, "No, no. These are just rumors. Everything is fine. I have it all under control." Margaret's eyes went to Noah, who nodded slightly.

Brian groaned and moved closer to Margaret, saying, "This is your fault. If you hadn't done what you did; if Tim hadn't—"

Noah interrupted him. "A change of plans. We're going to the film festival this weekend. Make an appearance. Take some photos."

Margaret added, "Rally our fans. Everything is going to be just fine."

Brian muttered under his breath, "This is bullshit. I've done too much to lose it now."

"Everyone, please," Margaret said in a not-so-chill voice.

"Those damn text alerts are poison," Fizz said. Brian had practically stopped eating a week before when the headlines said he looked like he was gaining weight.

Brian huffed and walked in circles. He went back to Margaret and said in a stern but calmer voice, "So you're saying these rumors aren't true?"

"That's precisely what I'm saying." Margaret's voice was tight yet calm.

Brian nodded, his jaw still clenched. "Better not be true." He cleared his throat. "I need some time to regroup. I'll go again after lunch," he said, walking out of the stables.

People exchanged worried glances.

"It's all good," Noah said, "I'll go talk to him."

"You're a hero," Haisley said to Noah, to which Fizz rolled his eyes.

"Let's take a break," Margaret said. "Keep your walkies on, and we'll resume filming shortly. We have to finish these scenes."

People dispersed.

Olivia stayed in the stables and read the rest of the article. It said that the show might be canceled, but the article's primary focus was on Brian's performance.

Damn.

It took her back to the gut punches she had received over the years. Critiques from film teachers, colleagues, well-meaning people who let opinions fly from their mouths like water from a hose. She remembered how sad she had felt when her thesis advisor had told her the film she had created her senior year was "fine, just not my taste." *Ouch.* Brian's fears were real, his anxiety, valid.

She pulled out her camera from its bag. "Let's go film some of this," she said to the camera.

Brian's trailer stretched along the grass between two smaller ones. Olivia approached it with the camera, recording.

From inside the trailer, she could hear Brian yelling, "I don't want to talk to anyone. This is my career. This is my life. None of you understand. Not even you."

She heard movement, then Noah said, "Get your shit together, man." His voice was deeper than usual, serious.

She caught a shot of the trailer and zoomed in on the door as it opened. Noah stepped toward her. A look of surprise flashed on his face when he saw her.

"He'll be fine in a few minutes," Noah said, his smile returning.

"Cool," Olivia said. "I'm just capturing some shots for the documentary I'm working on."

Noah squinted questioningly at her.

"Just for fun," Olivia said. "Margaret said it was okay."

"Okay. Give him some time. It's been a hell of a week," Noah said, walking past her back toward the stables.

When Noah was out of sight, Olivia knocked on the trailer door. "Brian, it's me, Olivia," she said hopefully. She held the camera tightly and bit her lip. "I'm working on a documentary of life on set, and I just want to capture a shot inside your trailer. It will show people how hard you're working." She had a feeling Brian might let her in if he knew she was working on something that could get him more positive press.

The door swung open, revealing a mess. Clothes were strewn everywhere. A hairdryer hung chaotically from a chair.

"Give me a minute to clean up," he said, moving things around.

Olivia nodded but pressed record. She zoomed in on the side of Brian's unkempt face.

"That's cool you're working on a documentary," he said as he moved a shirt off the back of a chair.

"Thanks," she said. She panned the camera away from Brian and toward his wardrobe. A row of plain T-shirts, blue jeans, a few pairs of overalls, and one suit hung from a rack. She moved toward the shelf of props he kept for his character: glasses, hats, boxes of varying shapes and sizes labeled with all kinds of things he might need to use. She zoomed in on them: Tylenol, garden sheers, some kind of horse medicine. He liked to choose his own supplies; he said it was all part of getting into character.

She moved the camera back on him and then clicked it off. With only one scene left to direct, she had to get through to him. She took a deep breath and tapped into the skills she had used with her students. "You're doing a great job, Brian." From working with students, she knew that empathizing and forming a bond could bring them closer together. "It must have been hard to read that article." He was only a few feet away, but he seemed somewhere else, far away.

Brian sat down in the makeup chair and rested his cheek on his hand. "Acting is all I have."

"You really have been doing a good job," she said.

"I need this to go well."

"I get that," she said. It was true. She understood the desire to succeed—to have financial stability, job security—all while doing something you love. Anything that threatened success or happiness, set off warning bells... And so, she listened like she had done so many times with her students. Their triumph was entwined, symbiotic.

"No one in my family thinks I can do this. They think acting is a waste of time. They tell me to do something useful. If I come home again with news like this..." he paused and shook his head. "I won't be able to face them."

Olivia sighed. "I know that feeling. But you're not disappointing anybody. You're doing a great job. I used to be a teacher, and I would tell my students that as long as they were trying hard and learning, mistakes would be part of the process."

"My mom's a teacher," Brian said. "Spends too much time at that damn school."

"She must be good then," Olivia said, smiling slightly.

"I think she's there to be away from my dad and brothers. Car mechanics can be tough to be around, loud and always talking about cars." Brian's tone was neutral, but there was a hint of sadness in his voice.

"Just keep doing what you're doing. Whatever it is, seems to be working. Your scenes this week have been amazing."

"You don't know what it's like to play Gregory Sky," he said, shifting his tone back to argumentative. His eyes glared ominously.

"You can shake this off. Do it for Tiffany," she said, choking up. Tears welled in her eyes, but she didn't want to cry, not again.

Brian's green eyes sharpened. He looked straight ahead; lips parted. "My career is the most important thing in the world to me. I won't let anything, or anyone, fuck that up." He spoke like a person issuing a warning.

Brian's desperation sent a chill through Olivia.

All this from one piece of media? Maybe Tiffany's death was affecting him in more ways than he was letting show.

Brian stood, "Let's go film the scene."

She followed him out of the trailer and back to the stables for the final scene of the week.

Olivia took her place beside Margaret.

Margaret uncrossed her arms. "Looks like we're good to go?" she asked.

Olivia nodded. "Are we all set here?"

"Equipment is ready," Margaret said.

Olivia exchanged glances with Haisley at the lights and Paige at the cameras. The women nodded, their faces calm.

Olivia stood a few feet from the actors. She could feel the raw emotion emanating from Brian like heat from the sun.

I'm going to push him to the edge of what he can feel.

This was her last chance. She took one final look at Margaret's eyes, assessing, grading.

"Okay, Brian," Olivia spoke. "You are the man. Remember, this woman has been using you, taking advantage of you, getting one leg up while you're on your ass."

Fire radiated from Brian's eyes.

Olivia monitored the faces of the male crew members nearby to gauge how well she was doing. Fizz stood frozen, transfixed.

So far, so good.

She sucked in a deep breath of air as the actors plunged into the scene. The red light from the camera blinked, capturing perfection. In the final moment of the scene, right on cue, Brian flung the shovel into the side of the stall. The steel echoed. The ground, following suit, vibrated beneath them.

Olivia beamed. Excitement cascaded through her.

"Well done, everyone," Margaret said happily. "That's a wrap for today. I'd like to see the fellows here for a brief meeting before the end of the day."

Haisley held out her hand, and Olivia accepted the high-five.

Margaret led them in a huddle. "Great job so far, ladies. You are doing excellent work here. I have some good news.

To thank you for your efforts, I was able to secure each of your short films a spot in the Jasper County Film Festival this weekend!"

"What?" Haisley cheered. "That's amazing!" Haisley put a hand on Olivia's shoulder. "This is huge." She drew out each word as if they were written in cursive.

People will see my film.

Feelings swirled inside her. On one hand, more exposure could lead to more conversations, more opportunities. On the other hand, if they thought her film was crap, she could ruin her chance of any future success.

The other women bounced. Their hands clasped into fists of excitement.

"Our projects will be out in the world," Paige said smiling.

"It's going to be a great opportunity. I'll see you tomorrow," Margaret said as she stepped away.

Tomorrow. Saturday.

Her stomach twisted. She took out her phone and texted Adira, "Can't make it tomorrow. Something came up. Reschedule for the following weekend?"

Adira texted back, "Film festival?"

Olivia held the phone in her hands, thumbs frozen in place, hovering over the buttons. She didn't want to lie to Adira, but she didn't want to invite her either. Sometimes the harshest critics are the people we care about the most.

"Yep," she texted.

Three dots wiggled back and forth.

"Following weekend is perfect."

Phew. Olivia exhaled. There was a chance Adira would see the film and love it, but Olivia wasn't ready to find out.

After everyone had left, Olivia flipped her camera open and panned across the empty stables. Steel metal and wood surfaces juxtaposed in the fading light. The door opened, and a woman walked in. She was middle-aged, maybe forty-five, hair in a tight bun, wearing light jeans and boots. She led a horse into the stall where the actors had been hours before. *So the property owners would be bringing the horses back for the weekend this time,* Olivia thought as she continued to film.

The woman examined the horse.

Olivia zoomed in on a gaping wound at the horse's neck.

The horse whinnied, and the woman shushed it, saying, "It will be all right, buddy. I'm going to get you all stitched up."

The woman went to a cabinet in the middle of the stable. She unlocked it and pulled out a plastic tray. She looked tired, weary. She walked back to the horse, which had continued bucking in the stall. She put a hand on the horse's neck, and the horse brought all four legs to the ground again. She whispered something in its ear. The horse stood still. Calm.

Olivia zoomed in.

The woman took the plastic thing in her hand—a needle—and plunged it into the horse's neck. The horse's head drooped.

Damn, what a great shot.

The woman, wearing a pair of medical gloves, got to work cleaning and then stitching the horse's neck.

Olivia closed the camera, smiling. The documentary was coming together nicely.

CHAPTER 23

Beep, beep, beep. The red lights of a food delivery truck blinked as it backed out of an alley between two shops. Olivia shifted on the bench. Her tailbone was sore from sitting for so long. Luckily, the shop owners on Main Street had begun flipping closed signs to open with the jingle of a bell, the cacophony of Saturday morning.

A man dressed in white painter's clothes pulled cans from the back of a van across the street. The air smelled of fried dough and hot oil. Regular people doing ordinary things felt odd to her today, like it was her birthday and she was hanging around people who were unaware.

"How are you feeling about today?" Jara asked from her side of the bench. In a black summer jumpsuit and her hair straightened, she looked like she was about to go on stage to accept an award.

"I'm excited," Olivia said matter-of-factly. Not that she wasn't excited; part of her was. But how she *felt* depended on how other people would react to her film. Sitting on the bench, waiting, Olivia's feelings were frying somewhere beneath the surface, pending. Contingent.

"How about you?" Olivia asked.

Jara flipped the page of the book on her lap. Looking up, she said, "Pretty good! Ready for it to get started."

Olivia nodded. The theater stood at the center of a row of local shops. They had names like Susie's Salads, Downtown Domestic, and Jasper Java and Donuts.

She took out her phone and flipped open a new tab on the internet browser. She typed the link to the film festival website. It popped up right away. She previewed the schedule: 10:00 a.m. first two shorts: Olivia Gabriel, Haisley Richards.

Olivia's stomach churned. As if she were playing a game of chess, she told herself she was making all the best moves. Joining the fellowship, directing the actors, working on a documentary of her own. But doing this, showing her film to hundreds of people, was a gamble. Like moving her queen to a risky check position, it could go either way. If it worked, she would win. If it didn't, if Margaret saw the improvements Olivia still had to make—all that she still had to learn—she could lose everything.

Two men unloaded a truck of boxes and carried them into Java and Donuts. A bus honked at a pedestrian who had walked into the road without looking. Without warning, a wave of electric fear zapped through her.

Fear was like that.

Sudden.

Unpredictable.

Her body begged her not to let them show her film.

Please, she ached, *don't put us through the torture of other people's opinions.* Letting other people see her film was like standing naked in front of them.

She was six again, standing in line for her first rollercoaster. "No, Dad, please don't make me. I don't want to go up that high."

"Kids love this stuff. You'll be glad you did it when you get up there."

Adrenaline coursed through her.

She didn't want to do this. She didn't want to expose herself in this way. Not now. Not when she was so close to winning a full-time spot. She had put in too much effort to lose it now.

Her heart thumped. The town clock struck nine, and bells played.

"You ready there, Sparky?" Jara asked.

Olivia looked at her, confused.

Jara shrugged. "I don't know why I called you that. My dad used to call me that when I was focused, and I guess you looked focused in that moment."

"Ah," Olivia said. "Cool."

Another bus pulled up, and Margaret, Haisley, and Paige stepped out. Noah and Fizz followed behind.

"You two overachievers couldn't wait for us?" Paige asked.

"We're all here now," Jara said. "Let's head in."

In the theater, artificial silk white wisteria hung from the ceiling along the aisles. The air conditioner blasted cold air from all angles. Olivia took a seat between Haisley and Margaret. She slunk back in the seat and squeezed her eyes shut for half a second.

The *whish* of air into a microphone blew from the speakers, and she opened her eyes.

A gray-haired man approached a stage at the front of the room beneath the screen. He adjusted the microphone and blew into it. He introduced himself as the moderator and said, "Congratulations to all our filmmakers on getting your projects into the world. We hope this experience gives you a chance to share your story and meet other people who will become your community along the way. We hope you enjoy today's experience. We'll get started shortly."

He clicked the microphone off, and advertisements scrolled across the screen as people mingled and made their way to seats. Vendors carried trays of popcorn and drinks through the crowd.

Haisley shifted in her seat. "Where is he?" She looked at her watch, head on a permanent swivel, checking for Al. "This is what I get for marrying a detective," she pouted.

Noah, who was huddled over a bag of popcorn on the other side of Haisley, said, "Don't worry about him. We're here for you."

Haisley smiled and grabbed a fistful of popcorn from the bag on Noah's lap.

As the theater went dark, Al jogged up the aisle, nearly knocking over a small woman with a cane, breathing heavy, "Sorry I'm late. We had a break in the case."

Everyone turned and stared at him.

Olivia's skin prickled with irritation. The too-strong smell of popcorn coupled with these people's disregard for the importance of the moment made her anxious.

Noah flicked a piece of popcorn into the air and caught it with his mouth.

"Can I get that seat?" Al asked Noah.

Noah didn't move.

"Haisley, come sit with me," Al pointed to open seats a few rows away.

Haisley rolled her eyes. "Just sit right there, and I'll come to join you when Olivia's film is done, and we can watch mine together."

Al's eyes were daggers.

Noah stood and said, "I'm just messing with you, man," and shuffled out of the row.

Al took Noah's seat, bumping Olivia's knees on the way past. She stifled a groan.

"Move it, dudes. It's about to start," Jara said.

"Where have you been?" Haisley demanded.

Al whispered to Haisley, "Sorry it took me so long. We just got the toxicology report back for Tiffany."

Tiffany. A new wave of nausea came over her. *What did the report say?* Curiosity nagged at her, but her film was about to start. She elbowed Haisley as kindly as possible. "Can you guys talk after this?"

Haisley turned to Al, put a hand on his thigh, and said, "Let's talk about it later."

The lights turned down, and the screen flashed with Olivia's title: *Imperturbable.*

On the screen, two birds flew over the ocean off the coast of Rhode Island, and then the image cut to the bones of a dead duck, head twisted sideways on the pavement. *Mary Oliver meets Mary Shelley.*

Olivia's eyes darted from the screen to the faces of the people around her. Everyone stared at the screen. Olivia couldn't read the expressions on their faces in the darkness.

The film rolled forward. The kid flew down the slide in a moment of gleeful innocence. The osprey dove from the perch. A cherry blossom stretched open in a time-lapsed clip like a toddler waking up from a nap. How natural for humans and animals to be playful.

Olivia flashed back to all the filming she had done walking through the park, standing at the ocean's edge, perching in the botanical gardens. She observed all these places through the camera, capturing beauty. But she had moved so quickly, always rushing through the filming to get to whatever came next—class, school, work, errands—that she hadn't fully appreciated the beauty of it all. Staring at it on the screen, she held her cheek with her palm. What had it smelled like at the ocean? How cold would the water have felt on her toes if she had dipped her feet in before rushing off?

The film cut to a shot of the duck pond on a dark and stormy day. Seeing the film again, Olivia heard her own message for the first time. *Experience life before it goes away.*

As her credits scrolled, her stomach dipped and rose like she was on a rollercoaster. The lights came up. She squeezed her fists under her legs.

The critique panel came to the front of the theater holding microphones. Three older men, good old boys, discussed her film like sports commentators. "I thought this film was well done. The use of imagery was especially effective."

The heavyset man shifted and adjusted his belt buckle. "What I would have liked to see is a stronger sequence, so we get a sense of the problem first and then the solution. I thought there were moments when this filmmaker jumbled the two. And maybe that was the point, but it didn't completely work for me."

The other men nodded in agreement.

Embarrassment draped over Olivia, making her whole body feel five times heavier.

The panel thanked the audience and shared a reminder to support independent filmmakers.

Olivia stared at her lap. The queen had made its move, and the opponent was still thinking. *Did Margaret like it?* She couldn't tell.

People shuffled in their seats for the five-minute break before Haisley's film.

Olivia turned to Margaret. "What did you think?"

"Good effort. It's good novice filmmaking. That's why I chose you for this fellowship."

Novice filmmaking. Olivia cringed. Her gut was on fire, and her body weighed a million pounds. She froze in the seat. Margaret had taken the queen and whacked it off the board. Checkmate.

Haisley leaned over to Olivia. "Great job. I enjoyed your film," she said, rubbing Olivia on the shoulder.

Whiplash.

Olivia had selective hearing when it came to feedback; she knew that. Something in her brain rerouted all the positive stuff to a secret tree somewhere off in the distance of a hidden forest. The you-can-do-better stuff was in her face, plastered to the inside of her brain like a collage. *Better sequence. Novice filmmaker.*

Her body cramped. *I should have stayed home.*

CHAPTER 24

The humid air outside the theater choked her. She learned that it was safer to keep people ignorant about her work; to be seen meant to be judged and criticized. Now, her film was no longer invisible. She felt vulnerable and exposed.

She stood under the canopy waiting for the others.

Some people had congregated by the bus stop while others trickled out of the theater and down the sidewalk. Standing next to the wall to the side of the entrance, Al leaned over and whispered something in Haisley's ear. Haisley's mouth fell open. She covered her face with a hand. Al and Haisley moved beneath the canopy.

Al said, "I better get back to work. Great job today." He hugged Haisley, waved goodbye to Olivia, and headed back toward his police cruiser parked on the opposite side of the street.

Olivia wanted to ask Haisley what Al had told her but decided to wait. It wasn't the right time—too many people. Jara and Paige emerged from the theater, and Haisley called them over. Margaret and Noah were right behind them, arm in arm.

Weird.

"We're going to head out," Noah said.

Margaret smiled, cheeks pink, and went off with Noah.

Olivia and Paige looked at each other.

"You didn't know about them? Those two have been together for a while," Haisley said. "Before filming started, they'd be working together at a Monarch all the time. Al and I saw them sipping milkshakes down at the local dairy."

Paige shrugged.

Olivia said, "No, I didn't know."

"Make a pretty good couple, I think. Mom and Pop," Haisley she said, chuckling. "Let's go get some drinks," she suggested. "Bar 17? We can celebrate our films and have a round of drinks in Tiffany's honor."

Bar 17. Olivia swallowed, unsure of how she felt about going back there so soon. *But*, she told herself, *being with friends would be better than being alone.*

Haisley ordered them a ride, and twenty minutes later they stood in the alley outside the bar.

Olivia's legs were pillars, unmovable.

"You okay?" Haisley asked. The women stood in a semi-circle around Olivia with concerned faces.

I don't think so.

"Yep," Olivia said, not moving. She wanted to take a step, but so much was happening in her mind that her body forgot what it was doing. Tiffany used to be alive, and then she wasn't. *This was the last place I saw her.*

"It will be okay," Haisley said. "Al is on it. Let's go in and get a drink, and I'll tell you what I know."

Jara and Paige nodded in support.

Haisley curled a friendly arm around Olivia and led her into the bar.

At the table, Jara ordered them a plate of nachos and a scorpion bowl. Then she cut to the question that Olivia wanted to ask: "Any updates on Tiffany?"

Haisley looked around the room. The place was about half full. An upbeat song played from the speakers. Still, Haisley leaned forward. Everyone else followed suit. Haisley whispered, "He said Tiffany's death was ruled a homicide. Said she was killed with a lethal dose of horse tranquilizer."

Olivia smelled bleach and asphalt. It burned like rubber inside her gut.

A waiter came by and dropped the food. "Everything okay over here, ladies?" he asked.

Olivia heard him, but she didn't respond. She felt dazed, as if she had spun in circles for hours. She replayed the news in her mind.

Tiffany was murdered.

What did that mean? Someone had *killed* her. It was all too shocking.

The other women must have been shocked because no one spoke. Everyone stared dumbly with their mouths hanging open, food and drink untouched.

Jara broke the silence, "I need a drink."

Olivia reached for a drink of water, and in her mind, she was falling on top of Tiffany's body. She shook her head, trying to snap herself out of the replaying memory. She touched the glass. It felt like the gate, cold in her hands. She swallowed a long, slow sip. The cold water slithered down her throat and into her stomach.

Anger rose within her. At least, she thought it was anger, hot and bitter. All the feelings cascaded, and she couldn't discern what was what in her mind and body.

"Horse tranquilizer?" Jara asked, confused.

Haisley shrugged. "That's what he said." She frowned and sat back in her chair. "Who could have done something like this?"

Olivia wondered that too. She remembered the horse with the gaping slash in its neck. But the horses hadn't come back on the weekend when Tiffany died.

"This is freaky, guys," Paige said.

They nodded in agreement.

"Who would want to hurt her?" Jara asked.

Everyone shrugged. Olivia shook her head and said, "I know the medicine is kept in the cabinet in the stables. I'm also pretty sure I saw a box of that tranquilizer on set somewhere." She pushed herself to try and remember where she had seen it, but she couldn't remember.

"You did?" Paige asked with a look of surprise.

Olivia nodded. "I'm pretty sure."

Haisley said, "If it came from Jasper, it should be easy to figure out who killed her. Right? Don't they have to keep track of drugs like that?"

Olivia frowned. "I would think so. They should at least be able to figure out where the tranquilizer came from."

Then it hit her—*the documentary footage.*

In her apartment, Olivia went straight to the clips she had filmed of life on set. She set the playback to be at two-times speed.

If she could find the box, and it was the one used to kill Tiffany, maybe they would want to keep her on as a location manager for the next show.

Her eyes burned from staring into the screen. She blinked back tears.

There it was on the shelf. The box. The label on the side read "XlaMed."

Olivia paused the video and zoomed in. The box said, "Xylazine 100 mg/mL injection. Sedative and analgesic for use in horses and Cervidae only."

Her heartbeat quickened in disbelief.

There it was.

In Brian's trailer.

CHAPTER 25

The sounds that seeped from the apartment above hers were not the usual sounds of arguments. The floorboards rocked gently back and forth. Creaking. A sound like a headboard tapping on the wall knocked in between creaks.

Creak. Knock. Creak. Knock.

Olivia set the laptop on the counter next to the empty bowl of cereal. The apartment was in near darkness. She hadn't bothered to turn on the lights. The time on the computer showed 10:35 p.m.

She flipped the lights on and unlocked the phone. She held it up to the laptop and recorded a few seconds of video. "I'll send it when he's done," she said to the tiger on the cereal box.

Moments of Brian on set replayed in her mind: his temper boiling over at the news that the show might be canceled, his insistence that no one understood him, the comments on set, "You don't know what it's like to play a character like Gregory Sky."

It must be hard to play a murderer. But wouldn't it be way more challenging to be *one?*

She slid into bed.

Creak. Knock. Creak. Knock.

She rested her eyes. When she opened them again, the clock read 7:29. Morning.

She dialed, and when Al answered, she said, "Hi. Al. I think I have something you may want to see." She texted him a recording of the video.

"Thanks, Olivia. We'll look into it."

The early morning quiet of her apartment screamed for her to seek the comfort of another person. Anyone. She got dressed and filled a cup of water in the tap.

She floated down the hallways and listened outside of each of the women's apartments for signs of life but didn't hear any.

Maybe they went to do some work and get ready for the week, she thought. She went outside and started the golf cart. It rumbled to life, and an involuntary shudder rolled through Olivia like a trembling volcano waking up from deep sleep.

What am I doing?

She pressed her foot on the gas and moved forward on autopilot.

At Jasper, she parked and went into the office.

"You okay?" Noah said from the computer, snapping Olivia from her daze. "You look exhausted."

He's working today?

She sat down in a chair. A few rebellious tears squirted from the corners of her eyes. "I'll be fine," she said. "It's just all so much."

Noah turned from the computer and joined her at the table.

Her body was heavy, leaden, but she forced herself to speak. "Tiffany is dead. I saw a box of horse medicine in my footage. Did the police come here yet?" Everything came out all at once, and she didn't know how to stop it. "I'm not going to win this job because Margaret doesn't like my video."

Noah's eyes widened. "What do you mean horse medicine?"

Olivia swallowed. "I went back through my footage and found a shot with horse medicine in Brian's prop collection. I think that might be what killed Tiffany."

Noah laughed in a quick, huffed gasp. "I think that really is just a prop," Noah said. "If he used it to hurt Tiffany, why would it be sitting on a shelf?" Noah looked away and mumbled something under his breath.

Olivia shrugged and put her head down on the table. *Maybe it is just a prop.*

"Which one of these problems is your biggest?" Noah asked in a low voice.

She lifted her head and cocked it to the side. "What do you mean? They all feel big."

"I mean, which one is making you the most miserable? Preventing you from being successful?" He spoke slowly in the same kind of voice she used when students weren't following directions.

Olivia scratched her forehead. What kind of question was that? Maybe he was trying to distract her. Which problem was the biggest? Her film? Her future? Her love life?

"I mean, aside from the fact that a few days ago I fell on top of a dead person, and in two weeks I might not have a job—" She paused.

In two weeks, I might not have a job.

Noah leaned forward in his chair and clasped his palms together. "Past and the future. Let's go to the present. What does success mean to you now? What, or who, is your biggest problem in the present?"

Olivia squinted at Noah, who apparently decided now would be the best time to show up and be her mentor. "I guess right now I want Margaret to hire me into a full-time position," she said.

Noah crossed his hands behind his head, cradling his neck. "My advice to you, kiddo," he leaned back in the chair, sending a wave of heavy cologne toward Olivia, "get rid of any obstacle that's in your way."

Olivia nodded. What were the obstacles in her way?

There was a knock at the door, and Margaret came in. "Hey, you two. A detective is here."

Margaret and Noah exchanged glances. Silence hung in the air. Olivia turned her head from Noah to Margaret and back again, trying to read the looks on their faces. Something passed between them like code teachers used when discussing things within earshot of students. As if they were keeping a secret.

"What's going on?" Olivia asked.

"They want to question Brian," she said, still looking at Noah.

Noah stood from the desk. "Better go help them out." He walked past Margaret out the door. She followed him.

Olivia unlocked her phone and opened a text. She added the women to a group message and wrote, "Police on set. Talking to Brian."

Haisley responded first, "I'm already here. Outside."

Olivia met Haisley outside.

"Al and another detective are going to ask Brian if they can search the trailer," Haisley said.

Across the yard, Olivia spotted the trailer. Al was a few strides from reaching Brian, who stood outside with his arms crossed staring up into the sky. Al wore a crisp suit, business-like rather than neon road biker. A woman walked a few paces behind Al.

They were too far away to make out the words, but Brian uncrossed his arms, nodded, and led them into the trailer.

"Do you think he did it?" Olivia asked. "Do you think Brian may have killed Tiffany?"

Haisley put a hand to her wrist, adjusting her bracelets. The silver glistened in the morning light. "No clue. I know he can be serious and get a temper sometimes, but I can't see him killing anyone. His character, Gregory, maybe. But not Brian. Fizz is much more of a psycho than Brian is."

"What do you mean?" Olivia asked.

"Nothing really," Haisley said. "Just a vibe."

Jara and Paige pulled up in a golf cart and joined them. "What's going on?"

As soon as she asked, Al and the other detective emerged from the trailer. The woman carried a zipped bag. Al turned and said something to Brian, but Olivia was too far away to hear. Brian shook his head and moved his hands like he was arguing. Then he tossed his head back in a gesture of disbelief.

"Are they arresting him?" Paige asked.

"Voluntary questioning, I think," Haisley said.

"Doesn't look voluntary," Paige responded.

"No handcuffs," Haisley said. "That boy is walking in on his own."

Brian and Al walked toward the police car, and Al opened the back door for Brian. Brian stepped in, arms free, without a fight.

Whoa. I did that, Olivia thought. She felt both proud and disturbed. What would happen to the show?

Our lead actor is a murderer.

CHAPTER 26

"What are we going to do without our lead actor?" Olivia asked.

"Don't worry," Jara said. "Margaret and I have worked out a kickass ending to this season that I think will be amazing. And we can use his stunt double to film it."

The women turned to Jara, who drifted toward the house. Jara stopped, turned back, and said, "We've all got work to do, and it will be great. I'll have the call sheets updated in an hour."

Great, Olivia thought. She couldn't believe they would still film the show after everything that had happened. At the same time, she knew they had to.

"Exciting!" Haisley said. "And reviews for our films should be out in the newspaper today." She shimmied her shoulders. "See you all tomorrow," she said walking away.

Olivia got back in the golf cart and drove home for her laptop. The flag outside Monarch Café blew in the breeze. She decided to stop for a coffee and a copy of the local paper. And Adira.

At the front of the store, Olivia peeked into the window, but she couldn't see past the condensation fogging the glass. If only everyone inside would hold their breath so that she could see for just a second. That's all the time she needed to find out if Adira was busy with a customer or alone restocking shelves of reusable cups and to-go snacks.

She stepped back from the window, a few steps from the door, and waited for a coffee-carrying customer to wander through the exit. She paced back and forth inches from the door. The chimes above the door shook, and Olivia jumped. No one came out of the store—false alarm. The hot summer wind had taken the opportunity to play a joke on her. *Very funny.*

The sun beat on her face like an interrogation lamp, forcing her to pull the door open. She strolled in and looked around.

Play it cool.

Two elderly customers read newspapers in leather chairs by a fake fireplace. Olivia's stomach ached, thinking that one of them might be reading a review of her film. She spotted Adira behind the counter steaming milk. The milk frother whistled.

Adira, striding back to the register, looked up and smiled.

Olivia smiled back, her mind relaxing in Adira's presence. She approached the counter.

"Large iced?" Adira asked, winking slightly.

"Actually, can I have a latte today? I'll stick around here this afternoon and get some work done."

"Of course," Adira said, moving to the steamer.

Olivia walked to the end of the counter, where Adira would meet her with the latte. She wanted to say more. Their last text exchange had been to reschedule the date. Olivia shifted without saying anything.

Adira passed the large ceramic mug toward Olivia. Her eyes glistened softly in the light bouncing off the silent steamer.

"Thank you," Olivia said. "Exactly what I need today."

Adira smiled and headed back to the register to help another customer.

Olivia took the drink and grabbed a newspaper from the stack. She found a cushioned seat in the corner and relaxed into it, wrapping her hands around the hot mug. A heart design, lines flawlessly drawn, smiled up at her. She opened the paper in her lap. The place was quiet, listening.

Olivia looked down at the paper, but her mind was on Adira. From the corner of her eye, she could see Adira moving deftly behind the counter. Olivia pretended to read the paper and pretended that the only thing running through her mind was the daily news. Her heart fluttered. She sipped the hot beverage.

Focus.

She searched the newspaper for the entertainment section, scanning rapidly for the film festival critiques. She stopped when she saw a picture of Margaret leaning over a camera at Jasper. Someone had been to the set.

Above the photo, the headline read: "Budget Cuts Force Cancellation."

All the air drained from the shop. Olivia gasped and bit her knuckle.

Damn.

Another rumor about the cancellation. A canceled show meant no job, whether she won the full-time spot or not. Unless Margaret had another project up her sleeve.

Olivia stared uncertainly at the black and white photo. Beneath the image, the article said:

"Production announced that this would be the final season for *Murder in Morristown*. Citing budget cuts, the production company, which had remained neutral as of last week, finally indicated that the show would likely be canceled."

Her eyes glazed over the page, and she blinked hard. She read on:

"It would take a miracle to keep the show alive, and some superfans are already praying for just that."

"Especially if Brian is arrested," Olivia muttered. Losing him would likely mean the end of the show.

Below the article, a group of people dressed in black held protest posters in front of the Hollywood sign. One frowning woman, hands pressed into a prayer position, dangled a sign from her elbows that read: "Don't cancel my show."

Olivia picked at the wet napkin underneath the cup. She remembered Margaret's response to the first published article with rumors of cancellation. Margaret had said things were going fine. She said they wouldn't be canceled if the actors performed well. *Could this article be accurate, or is it just more gossip?*

Olivia swallowed. The heart design in the cup had blurred into an indiscernible puddle.

She set the paper down on the table.

"Want some company? I've got a ten-minute break." Adira sat in the chair beside her. "How was the festival?"

Olivia's heart thrummed fast but softly; in Adira's presence, worries faded to the background. "Pretty good," Olivia said. "I'm not sure it was worth missing out on time with you, though."

Adira smiled. "It seems like you don't have much time outside of work right now."

"I might have *too* much time soon if this news is true," she said pointing at the headline. "Looks like we really might be canceled soon."

Adira looked down at the paper. "Your job is really important to you, huh?"

"It's my dream," Olivia said.

"Couldn't you find another project to work on?"

"Working in film is a lot different than serving people coffee. They don't just exist on every corner." The words flew out of her mouth before she could stop them. As soon as she saw the look on Adira's face, she wished she could take them back.

"That's not what I meant. Adira, I—" Olivia smacked herself on the forehead. "I truly didn't mean it how it sounded."

"It's all good." Adira turned. "I've got to get back to work anyway. Got to make sure the people have their coffee," she said in a tone Olivia couldn't read. Was she upset?

Olivia fumbled for words.

What am I doing?

The stress of everything came down on top of her.

Adira turned and moved back to her place behind the counter. She wiped down the same machines she had cleaned a few minutes before.

Olivia sighed and tucked the newspaper under her arm. She wanted to follow Adira to the counter, but she didn't know what to say. She took the coffee and walked out the door. As the door chimed behind her, Olivia's thoughts beat against her head: *You're not doing enough. You're not enough. You fucked it up again.*

Tears clawed at the back of her eyes as she ascended the creaking stairs to the apartment.

Back inside, Olivia tried to convince herself that this too would pass and that everything would be okay. But she wasn't sure. She unfolded the newspaper and flipped to the page about the film festival. She scanned the page of reviews, intent on finding a review of her film. She got to the end. Not a mention.

She went back to the review of Jara's film. "Unique, original, fresh. This girl is one to watch."

Olivia ripped up the paper and threw it in the trash. She felt like she was on the ground floor of a toppling building. Everything was crumbling around her. For so many years, she had listened to the people who told her things would be okay. The teachers who had said that a person as tenacious as she would be just fine.

If only they could see her now.

She opened the laptop. While she was working on the call sheets, a text came through the group chat.

Haisley: Brian was released. It wasn't him.

CHAPTER 27

A faint rumbling sound rose over the hum of the laptop. Olivia stopped typing and listened. Voices came from Haisley and Al's apartment, getting louder. She strained to make out the words, but they were jumbled.

Things quieted, and Olivia went back to the call sheets, trying to calm her mind by throwing herself into work. If Brian didn't do it, a murderer was still out there. Olivia reviewed the notes for the final scene. At the top of the document, Margaret had left a comment: "For the director and crew only. I will prepare the actors in real-time."

Listed under the first assistant director, Olivia read her name. She choked back tears of joy. Margaret had given her another scene.

Olivia clicked the link to the final script. She read each word, soaking in the ending that Jara had written. When she got to the end of the scene, her mouth dropped open.

She opened her phone and texted the group. "Shit. I can't wait to see his reaction. Nice job, J."

Jara: "Thanks!"

Olivia shuddered happily as she reread the scene. *Nice.*

She prepared her notes until late into the night. At two minutes after midnight, shouts came from upstairs. Concern grew as she tried to make out the words.

"What's going on up there?" she asked the cardinals.

She stood and paced in the kitchen. *Maybe I should go up there,* she thought, *just in case.*

She texted Haisley, "You good?"

Something shattered against the floor above Olivia's head.

She put on her sneakers, didn't bother tying them, and threw on a sweatshirt. She couldn't do anything to help Tiffany, and she wouldn't sit around and let something happen to Haisley.

The hallway smelled like the usual, rotting eggs. Both the stairway and the elevator were at the opposite end of the hallway. Olivia walked quickly down the gray hallway and took the stairs to Al and Haisley's floor. Everything was quiet when she got to Al and Haisley's apartment door. She checked her phone to see if Haisley had responded. Nothing. She tapped on the apartment door. No response.

Her heart drummed like a jackknife in her chest. Had they gone out? They could have taken the elevator or gone down the stairs in the time it took Olivia to get dressed and up there.

She dialed Haisley's number. It rang in her ear—and behind the door.

Olivia opened a text to Jara and Paige. "I'm worried," she started, and then she erased the message and called Jara instead.

"Hey, I'm worried about Haisley," Olivia said. She explained the situation.

"Okay. I heard it too, but they always fight. Sometimes they leave after they fight to cool off. Type in the apartment code. Four-four-two-four. Haisley gave it to me when I had to drop off her cart keys."

Olivia punched in the code. She looked around the apartment, but it was dark. "I don't see anyone." She turned on the lights and went inside. A vase of coins lay shattered on the floor.

She tiptoed past and checked the bedroom. No one was home.

"They probably just went out to cool off," Jara said calmly.

Olivia closed the door to the apartment and retreated to her own. "What do you think we should do?"

"I don't think we need to do anything, but we could go out and look for her if you're worried."

Olivia took a moment to think. If something happened to Haisley, and she didn't do anything about it, she didn't know if she could live with herself. The memory of the drowned girl floating in the pool swam in her mind. "Where would she go this time of night?"

"Bar 17? Jasper? She and Noah are pretty close. Maybe she would have gone to him?"

"I'll call him. Maybe they're together."

"Okay. Text me if you hear from her," Jara said.

Olivia jogged back to her apartment and dialed Noah. *Ring. Ring. Ring.*

"Hello?" Noah spoke as if he were out of breath.

"Hey Noah," Olivia said, trying to stay calm. "Have you seen Haisley?"

"Not since earlier. It's the middle of the night. She's probably home sleeping like you should be."

Olivia heard noise from Noah's end of the line. "Where are you?" she asked.

"At the hotel. Get some sleep, Olivia. I'll see you in the morning."

Olivia hung up the phone quickly. Uneasiness crept over her.

That was strange.

Olivia's mind raced. She called Al, but the phone went to voicemail.

She took off her shoes and sat on the bed, thinking. A few minutes later, the ringing phone interrupted her thoughts.

Al.

"What's up?" he asked.

"Is Haisley with you?" Olivia suddenly felt uncomfortable. "Is everything okay?"

"Everything's fine. I'm dealing with a case. Haisley should be home by now."

"Last time I checked, your apartment was still empty."

Silence hung between them for a moment.

"She said she was going back to the worksite to get something she forgot. Cool off a little bit. But she should be back." He paused as if he were thinking and then said, "Can you go check on her?"

"Yep," Olivia said. "I'm on it."

Upstairs, the apartment was still empty. She texted Jara, "Al hasn't seen her. I'm going to check Jasper."

"Sounds like a plan," Jara texted.

A slight nervousness crept over her. Something didn't feel right. She grabbed the keys to her golf cart and headed out into the night.

CHAPTER 28

After riding in darkness, Olivia thought she would be happy to see the distant glow of light coming from the farmhouse, but instead, it filled her with dread. Something wasn't right.

She parked the cart outside the gate. Her hand shook as she typed in the code. The sky was clear and dark; all the heat drained from Earth. She left the cart on the road and stepped forward. Gravel crunched beneath her feet as if she were breaking ten thousand potato chips with each step.

She stopped about ten feet from the house. The window to the living room on the left side of the main door was open a crack. She peered through the window. No one sat on the long floral sofa. A man about Noah's size and stature stood in the shadow just beyond the glow of a bulbous table lamp.

On the floor, a woman lay unmoving in a pool of light. Haisley.

Okay, Olivia, she thought, *stay calm.* This was an issue for the damn police.

She gasped for air, but she couldn't breathe.

I've got to help her.

She scanned the area. Noah's car was parked next to a blue one that Olivia didn't recognize. She snapped a photo.

Do something.

She inched forward through the grass toward the window that was just higher than eye level. She maneuvered behind a manicured tea olive bush, staying out of view should anyone peer out into the night.

The windowsill, painted white, rubbed against her fingers. Her biceps strained as she pulled herself up. A man sat on a leather armchair in front of a wall of books with hands pressed to his bald head. Fizz. What was he doing there?

Olivia's arms ached as she repositioned herself in the window.

The man in the shadows stepped into the light. He paced back and forth in front of Haisley.

Noah.

What the hell is going on here?

She stepped away from the window, slid her phone from her pocket, and stared at the screen. The phone hopped in her hand like a jumping bean. She took a deep breath, but her hands continued to shake.

Calm down.

She could no longer maintain the still, calm, patient exterior. She was ice, cracking, a thawing pond.

What the fuck do I do?

She glanced back through the window. Haisley's eyes were open, blinking, but she didn't get off the floor. Olivia breathed a sigh of relief.

It's not too late.

Fizz moved next to her, gazing at her. Noah walked toward him.

Olivia went back to the window.

"What are we going to do?" Fizz asked in a low, panicked voice.

"You're going to do what you need to do to solve your problem," Noah spoke loud and clear.

Olivia's mouth fell open hearing his words.

"I came here for a few drinks with a friend, not to *murder* someone." Fizz's voice was tight, serious. He kept his volume down as if someone might overhear them.

"You've been complaining for weeks that you don't want to be upstaged by some young gaffer. A woman, no less. Now is your chance. Do something about it."

Fuck.

Olivia let go of the window. The bush prickled against her arms and legs. She ran around to the side of the house out of earshot of the window.

Her interactions with Noah replayed in her mind. *What's the biggest obstacle in your way?* Brian's comment to her in the trailer sounded so similar. *I won't let anything or anyone get in my way.*

She took the deepest breath she could muster and called Noah.

The ringing shrilled in her ear.

Pick up. Pick up. Pick up.

"Hello?" Noah answered.

Good.

Olivia cleared her throat. She spoke in the calmest, warmest voice, "Hey Noah. We still haven't seen Haisley, so wanted to see if you heard from her in the last few hours?"

"Why don't you check the bars? You know how Haisley is. She's probably out drinking and flirting." Noah's voice was even and relaxed, sending shivers down her spine. She needed to find a way to stall him.

"Okay, will do. Thank you," she said. Then she added, "I'm going to send Al down to Jasper to look for her."

She hung up the phone and returned to her spot at the window to ensure Haisley was still okay. She was, at least for now. Noah and Fizz were back on the couch. Their arms moved in conversation.

Olivia tucked herself back into the spot by the window. She held her breath.

Noah and Fizz spoke like two men in a bar.

"You have to do this," Noah said.

"This isn't right, man," Fizz said. He wiped beads of sweat from his bald head. "I can't do this."

"For weeks, you've been telling me she's been a problem for you." Noah opened a box and pulled out a small bottle of solution. Olivia recognized it instantly. "The best way to solve a problem is to get rid of it."

Olivia sprinted away from the house and called Jara. "You've got to get help now. Call Al," she panicked. "I'm going in there."

She hung up the phone and rushed toward the house. She ran straight to the door and knocked.

Noah opened the door. "Well, isn't this a surprise?"

"What's going on here?"

"Why don't you come inside, and we can figure this all out."

Before Olivia could say anything, his hand was on her arm, yanking her into the house. Something struck her head. Then darkness.

CHAPTER 29

Olivia blinked her eyes open and looked around the room from her spot on the floor.

"Olivia...are...you...okay?" Haisley gasped from the spot next to her.

Her arm throbbed where Noah had pinched, and her tailbone ached.

"I think so," Olivia whispered. Her body writhed in pain. "What's going on?"

The door to the living room was closed. Fizz and Noah's voices no longer echoed from the hallway.

Silence.

"I came over to see Noah, maybe have a drink. Fizz was here when I got here. Both reeked of vodka. Did you call anyone?"

"I think Al is on his way here. I called Jara too."

Haisley gasped. "I'm scared."

"Me too. We need to buy some time." Olivia's heart rapped in her chest, and sweat beaded on her forehead. She moved, and a bolt of pain shot down her arm.

The door opened and Noah walked in, followed by Fizz, who closed the door quietly as if not to wake a sleeping child.

"Now we have two problems," Noah said.

You're the only problem.

Noah stepped toward her. He licked his crusty lips. She could tell by his pacing that he didn't have a plan. At least, not one he felt sure about. He tapped the small box against his palm—the same type of box that had been in Brian's trailer.

Horse tranquilizer.

Think, she told herself. From what she could gather, Noah believed that if Fizz killed Haisley, his problem would be gone. She thought about the conversations she had overheard between Brian and Noah. Always problem-solving, Noah refocusing Brian on the next scene. Was this what happened to Tiffany? Is this what he was trying to get her to think about during his single moment of mentoring? Olivia felt her mind go into overdrive.

By his own logic, if she could convince Noah that *he* was the problem, would his attention move away from Haisley?

"You're the biggest problem in my way," Olivia said.

"Everything is your biggest problem, Olivia," he said. His eyes bulged.

"No, really. If I want to be the location manager and that's your job, then aren't you my biggest problem?" She studied his face. The gray hair on his face, tiny quills, twitched. He looked like a different person than the man she first met. Older somehow. There was an anger within him bristling to the surface.

He picked at his chin. "What should I do about it?" He opened the box and pulled out the vial. From his briefcase on the couch, he procured a needle.

Olivia choked on a deep breath of air and tried to regain a steady rhythm. She coughed, and pain coursed through her.

"You're right," he said. He held the needle an inch from his arm. Haisley gasped and Fizz jumped up.

What was he doing? This wasn't what she had in mind.

"No," she gasped.

"What the hell, man?" Fizz said.

"Got to solve the problem," Noah said like a determined child sitting in front of a math worksheet.

"Wait." He might be joking, she couldn't tell, but she didn't want anyone to die. Not Noah, not Tiffany, not Haisley, not her brother Billy. "I have to tell you something first."

Noah perked up and let his hand relax away from his arm. Fizz sat back down in a ball on the couch beside him like a tired dog.

Outside, the world was dark. Olivia thought she heard the faint crunch of gravel.

"If you were gone, I wouldn't have a mentor. So, it would be a problem for me if you weren't here." She spoke slowly, letting each word fall one at a time. "When I was little, I lost a mentor. My brother taught me everything about life. How to burp on command. How to get something from Mom if Dad said no."

Olivia's breathing slowed with each word. While she spoke, she lost touch with reality; it was as if she were standing at the center of an expansive, frozen lake, talking to the mountains.

She locked eyes with the man in front of her.

"He taught me the important things too. How to ignore anyone who told me that I threw like a girl and to throw fast pitches by them anyway. How to take my time with the books I enjoyed and speed up through the tedious homework."

She paused.

Noah's face was blank.

There was so much more she would have learned from Billy if he had made it past sixteen.

"If you're gone, Noah, I won't learn everything I need to learn to be successful here."

Noah erupted in a fit of bubbly, hysterical laughter.

Olivia looked at Haisley, who nodded as if to say, "Keep going."

A crash came from outside, followed by the glitter of blue lights.

"I can't believe you thought we would hurt you," Noah stared blankly.

"We were joking. This was all a game," Fizz said.

Noah shook his head and looked at Fizz. "He didn't have it in him anyway."

The door opened, and Al barged through. "What's going on in here?" he asked. Al made his way toward Noah.

Olivia exhaled. *Thank God.*

A dark-haired woman with soft hands helped Olivia stand.

"I'm going to walk you out to the ambulance so they can check you out. You're going to be okay."

Olivia cried involuntarily. "I'm sorry," she said.

"It's going to be okay," the woman repeated. "You're okay."

She didn't feel okay. Her head pulsed, and she couldn't find her breath. There was an arm around her. Haisley.

"Thank you," Haisley said.

She stepped forward with Haisley out into the night. In the back of the ambulance, someone draped a blanket over her shoulders. EMTs in blue suits asked for her name and date of birth. She answered their questions between sips of water. Someone scraped beneath her fingernails. She heard the words "crime scene" and "attempted murder" and "two women."

Behind the EMTs, Olivia spotted Noah being led in handcuffs to the police car. Fizz too.

As they drove away, the convulsion of tears turned into a trickle. The fear that had coursed through her all night began to drain.

She still had that chokey, post-cry breathing when she saw Adira.

"How'd you get in here?" Olivia asked. "They said only family were allowed."

"Apparently, 'girlfriend' was enough," she said smiling.

Olivia's skin tingled in a good way. Adira wrapped her in a hug.

"They said that after they ask you a few more questions, you can go home. Do you want to come home with me tonight? You can get some rest, and in the morning I'll serve you coffee." She winked.

"Ha ha," Olivia said sarcastically, really appreciating Adira's sense of humor. The thought of being alone was almost too much for her to bear. "I'd love to come home with you."

CHAPTER 30

A kettle whistled. A sweet, sugary smell filled the air. Olivia sat up. The bed wasn't hers. The plush comforter was soft and warm, white. She brought her knees to her chest and listened. Light streamed through translucent curtains. Outside the window, a birdfeeder hung from a post in the garden, and a cardinal perched on top of it.

Olivia crawled out of bed, body aching. She wore a sweatshirt and pajama pants, neither of which belonged to her. *That's right. Adira.*

She wandered into the kitchen. The room was wide-open and bright. The ceiling stretched high, and light poured onto the white countertops.

Adira held the kettle. "Morning, sunshine," she said.

"Morning," Olivia said wearily. The timer above the oven beeped, and Olivia jumped.

"It's okay. Just the timer," Adira said, smiling softly. Olivia relaxed.

Adira went to the oven and pulled out a coffee cake. She set it down on a cooling tray and hugged Olivia. "Rough night. Were you able to get some sleep?"

Olivia sat on a stool at the counter and wiped the crust from her eyes. "A little." The need for urgent help vanished, and in its place came a subtle nagging that maybe her life could use some tweaks.

"You can stay here for as long as you want," Adira said, as if she could read Olivia's mind.

"Thanks," she said. She rubbed her sore, tired eyes; nightmares haunted her mind. "I can't believe everything that happened last night."

"We don't have to talk about it if you don't want to," Adira said, brushing wisps of hair off her face. "But I'm here if you want to talk." Adira handed her a mug of coffee. "Pour-over. My specialty," she said, winking. "I hope you like it."

Olivia wrapped her hands around the hot mug and soaked in the nutty smell. "Unless my brain was playing tricks on me, Noah tried to get Fizz to *kill* Haisley."

"That's what I gathered too from what people were saying."

"Why would he do that?" Olivia wondered out loud.

Adira shook her head, taking a seat on a stool. "I'm not sure. He's been a little weird since last year when his dad died. They used to do everything around town together: manage all the properties, all the horse farms, everything. You know, Noah's mother was a Jasper. Caroline Jasper? Family pretty much owns the town."

Olivia shook her head. "Wow, no, I didn't know that."

Adira rubbed Olivia's back with her fingertips. "Yeah, you never know what's going on with people under the surface."

Olivia nodded.

So true.

Noah had been so focused on solving problems, maybe stemming from his own pain. Everyone seemed to be determined to create their own versions of success without much thought of how that would impact the people around them.

For so many years, she, too, had focused on the wrong things, sacrificed friends and relationships for work and validation. What would it be like to have a good life outside of work? A life with friends and a partner?

It's time to make some changes.

On the counter, Olivia's phone and keys sat among a few apples in the fruit bowl. She checked her phone. An email message from Margaret. "No filming today. Will do last scene Tues + announce fellow winner + wrap early." The whole message was in the subject line; there was nothing else in the body of the mass email sent to all cast and crew. No mention of the incidents. How could she be so cold?

Olivia read the message to Adira. "What do you think is wrong with this woman?"

"I don't know, but something seems off. Do you think you'll go?" Adira slid a plate toward Olivia.

Olivia stuck her fork into the cake. "I don't think so. I'm supposed to help with the scene, but I might just tell her I don't want to. I don't think I can do it right now."

"That's understandable. I wouldn't be ready to go back to work if I experienced everything you've been through."

Olivia nodded. A piece of cinnamon coffee cake melted on her tongue. The opportunity to be part of *Murder in Morristown* had pushed her back to a place of insecurity. She didn't trust her own opinion, so she relied on the opinions of others. *I still want to tell the stories that need to be told.*

She tossed the thought around in her mind. She didn't have to go back, but part of her wanted to finish what she had started. Find her way back to herself.

"Actually, I think I'll go tomorrow and be there for the last day. I've been working on something: a documentary. It's something that I wanted to do, similar to a journal, you know, documenting life on the set. But I think it could be something more. Maybe I can show it to you sometime."

"I'd love to see it."

Olivia smiled and went over to Adira. She wrapped her arms around her and leaned forward. Adira's lips were soft and sweet, coffee and cake.

"I'd love to show it to you."

CHAPTER 31

Adira drove up to the gate, and Olivia walked down the path toward Jasper Equestrian for the last time.

Olivia strapped the handheld camera to her wrist so tight that it stayed in place without her holding on. She pressed record. The morning sky, black and sinister, glared down on the stables and farmhouse. There were remnants of yellow tape draped from trashcans, the last remaining signs that a crime scene crew had been there.

She turned off the camera. Inside the house, she skipped past the living room in a near-run. Voices came from behind Margaret's closed office door. She stood against the cold plaster wall in the hallway and listened.

"Are you ready for the scene?" Margaret spoke. All business. Always.

"Yes," Brian responded in a worn voice.

"This is a big scene, and I haven't told you much about it yet because I want you to act naturally. We want to capture your authentic reaction."

"You're killing me off the show?" Brian asked astutely.

Silence.

"That's fucked up," Brian said. "After everything you and I have been through, you're killing me off the show?"

Olivia didn't move. She heard papers rustling.

"It's for the best," Margaret said. "You'll find something new. I'll start a new show. We could both use a fresh start, don't you think?"

Silence stretched the length of the farmhouse.

"Your boyfriend turned me into a monster," Brian said. "I'll never forget seeing you and Noah standing over Tim in that dank studio kitchen. Heart attack, pfft," Brian spat. "I know what you two did to him."

"Brian, please," Margaret's voice was cool and calm despite the accusation. "It's all over now. I've handled the Tiffany situation."

Brian's voice grew louder. "I did what I had to do to get into character. That's what you told me to do. That's what Noah told me to do. Do whatever it takes to succeed. You don't know how hard that was for me. Pretending to be something that I'm not." Brian spoke in an intense, choppy manner.

Olivia shivered. She remembered her conversation with Brian on set, coaxing him to dig deep to perform. Brian's words played in her head, sending shivers down her back. *"You don't know what it's like to play Gregory Sky. What it's like to play a murderer."* He had taken getting into character to a whole new level.

"And if Noah opens his big mouth and says anything, my career will be over," Brian said in a low voice.

The crunch of gravel came from outside—the twinkle of blue lights. Al emerged from the car with a hand on his holster.

Olivia scampered to the kitchen and started a pot of coffee, pretending to be busy. From down the hall, she heard, "Brian O'Sullivan, we're going to need you to come with us. You're under arrest for the murder of Tiffany Wilson."

"Why don't you take her too. She knew about this."

"We pay you to perform, Brian. And by your actions, it seems like that's what you're still doing," Margaret said, voice cool.

"Let's go, Brian. It's time."

Olivia poured coffee into a mug. Her tailbone ached, and she arched her back. Thoughts spun in her head.

"Oh, good. Glad you made coffee. I'm gonna need some," Haisley said, opening the cabinet and grabbing a mug from the shelf. She had a bruise on her arm just below her elbow that matched Olivia's.

"What's going on out there?" Olivia asked.

"Ugh, nothing good. I doubt we'll be doing much more in this place after today." Haisley sipped coffee. "Margaret just sent one of those subject line only emails. We're going right to panel interviews today. They're taking filming back to the studio in Reno."

Olivia nodded. "Makes sense."

They walked together to the upstairs parlor where, according to the thorough preparation email from JD, the fellow interviews would take place. Olivia rearranged the books and set the camera on the shelf. With the fellows' permission, she would capture their responses to the interview questions.

Back in the office, she reviewed the email with directions for the panel interviews. It contained a sample of possible interview questions: Why do you want to work on this team? What is your definition of an effective story? What vision would you bring to the show?

Olivia folded her hands, elbows pressed against the desk, and stroked her eyebrows with her thumbs. Back in film school, hunkered down with her peers in a half-dark library filming room, scribbling notes in a notebook while a movie clip played, she was happy. Life was simple. She would debate with classmates if a symbol was a symbol or just an accident, like the stake and other objects as phallic symbols in *Dracula* or the use of light and darkness in *Frankenstein*. Together they created short films and shared them with students at other schools. They were on a mission to do nothing but learn and create, and the process was fun.

What changed? The summer hadn't been all fun and creative. It had been stressful and hard.

She chewed on her top lip and practiced her responses to the possible questions: *I love film because I love that there are endless ways to express an idea. When life gets confusing, the process of making a film helps me untangle the questions and piece together the answers. The process of shooting, editing, creating, is fun.*

She yawned.

More coffee.

She went to the kitchen and started another pot. As it brewed, she continued to consider what she might say to the panel. She started to wonder if there were certain answers the panelists would be looking for. They likely had an answer key that was more difficult to figure out than flipping to the back of the teacher manuals she used to use.

The women met in the parlor and took their seats in front of the three interviewers: Margaret, a judge she recognized from the festival, and another white-haired guy.

"Welcome, ladies," Margaret spoke, hands folded on a notepad. "Thank you for your hard work this season. It's been a pleasure to have you on the set. Each of you contributed in a meaningful way, and we're grateful for your work. But, as you know, we only have room in the budget to take on one more full-time member. While it likely won't be this show, we have others in the works. You've all done exceptional work, and now we want to ask you a few questions to make sure our selection is the top candidate and a true fit for our team."

Olivia clasped her hands on her thighs. *Top candidate? True fit? What did those words mean?* The hard seat pressed uncomfortably into her back. How could Margaret keep going on like this? Emotionless and indifferent. Careless.

"As you can see," Margaret continued, "I'm joined by my colleagues here. We'll serve as a team making the final decision together."

Do I really want to be part of a team like this?

The panel took turns asking the questions. When it was her turn, Olivia provided the answers she had rehearsed. From time to time, she peeked at the bookshelf as she listened to the graceful responses of her peers. Jara insisted she would still happily accept the title of "winner" even though she was honest about her plans to accept a job elsewhere at the end of all of this. Paige, picking at her nails, thanked them profusely and outlined her vision for a new star to arise in season three, where she would turn the murder mystery into a hopeful drama. With a replacement lead actor, of course.

When they got to Olivia, she looked across the panel. Her heart felt heavy. Where she expected to feel excitement and adrenaline, there was emptiness. She looked at the taller man who wore an argyle bowtie and the other in the tweed coat.

She looked down the row at her peers. Her friends. The gentle eyes of the women sitting alongside her encouraged her to speak. She remembered that first day together and how nervous she had felt to share herself with them.

She addressed the panel. "Thank you for this opportunity. I've learned a lot from this experience. Whether I win the competition or not is up to you, but I don't want to leave here without sharing."

She paused and stood, taking the camera out of its spot behind the bookshelf.

"While I would love to continue working on the show, I'm most passionate about creating stories that are real. I made a documentary of life on the set that I hope to produce after this is all over."

The taller man spoke, "If this is a trick, that's not really the way to go about winning, young lady. And spending company resources to create your own film is unprofessional, in my professional opinion."

"I used my personal resources; Margaret gave me permission to film," Olivia responded. She felt calm, certain that she had done the right thing.

Margaret shifted in her seat. "This is a huge opportunity for one of you. I'd hate to see you throw it all away."

Olivia shook her head. Margaret wasn't the type of person for whom she wanted to work. This wasn't the place for her.

More opportunities will come.

The air in the room was stuffy, uncomfortable. Frowns of disapproval stretched across the faces of the panelists. But Olivia felt calm. A voice from inside said, *I approve.*

I approve.

"Excuse me," she addressed the room, "I'm going to withdraw from this competition. Thank you again for the opportunity." She smiled at Jara, Haisley, and Paige and left the room.

Outside she found a quiet place under a tree beside the stables. She took a deep breath and let the tears fall. Tears not of sadness, but of relief.

A little while later, Jara, Haisley, and Paige stood in front of her.

"You okay?" Jara asked, taking a seat on the ground cross-legged in front of Olivia. Knee-to-knee. "You didn't miss much back there."

Olivia nodded. They didn't have to come, yet they did. A special kind of feeling washed over her. "Thanks for coming."

Paige and Haisley joined them on the ground.

"The last few weeks have been pretty tough for everyone," Jara said.

"I'm not sure we really got what was advertised," Paige said.

Olivia pressed her hand against her eyelids to soothe her eyes. Being in their company, she felt better.

"I promise, things around here usually aren't this eventful," Haisley said. "Congratulations on winning, Jara. Do you think you'll accept?"

"I'm going to think about it."

"That ending was incredible," Olivia said.

"It really was," Haisley agreed. "I think I'll stick to advertising for now. I miss my team back there."

"How about you, Olivia? Are you going to go back to teaching?"

Olivia bit the inside of her cheek and uncrossed her legs.

"I'm not sure yet," she said truthfully. "I still need some time to think." She yawned. "I could use a few weeks' sleep, I think."

The women laughed and nodded in agreement.

She wanted them to know how much their friendship meant to her. It was hard to say out loud, but she took a deep breath and said, "I'm so happy to have met you all. Even though our time was cut short, I hope we can stay in touch and maybe even work together again."

"Definitely," Jara said.

Paige and Haisley nodded in agreement.

Whatever she did next, she would take a break first. But she would do her best to stay in touch with her new friends. Healing from the chaos was more important than success.

CHAPTER 32

In the quiet of morning, sitting at Adira's kitchen table, Olivia pieced together footage of her moments on set: the horse's vocal anguish, actors performing, Margaret's desperate attempts to finish a TV show started by her husband.

What would happen to Margaret, anyway? According to the obituary, Tim died from a heart attack.

Leave it to Brian and the detectives to work that out.

She reviewed the scenes, people yearning for success. What would happen if, as a society, we all relaxed? Stopped performing?

When the documentary was complete, she went outside. In the garden, birds chirped. Sunflowers blossomed near the vibrant grass.

Adira stood at the front of a magnificent, white oak shed the size of a small cottage. Olivia approached her and wrapped her in a hug.

"Welcome to the studio," Adira said, sliding open the wide doors. Light poured through the windows.

Olivia took her camera out of the bag and flipped off the cap. She filmed a close-up shot of the glazed ceramic pots lining the shelf—Adira's studio.

Voices rose behind her. Jara, Haisley, and Paige walked toward Olivia and Adira.

"Welcome, everyone," Adira said. "Glad you could make it." Adira directed the women to their spots behind the wheels. "I was able to borrow some equipment from the studio downtown, so you each have a station." With the doors open wide, the studio was like an outdoor classroom.

Adira cut hunks of clay using a wire rope and set one down on each wheel.

Paige poked at one with a black nail.

Jara put both hands on her clay right away. "Okay, now, I've done this before, but you're going to have to take it slow for Paige over here." They all laughed.

"We have all day," Adira said, smiling into the camera. "First, everyone, get a cup of water and get to know your tools."

Haisley played with a plastic, scalpel-like tool. "Do we have to use our hands?"

"It will be fun, Haisley," Jara said. "If you break a nail, we'll get you another one."

"Ha, ha," Haisley responded playfully. "I have an appointment tomorrow just in case." She tapped her head, "Thinking ahead."

Adira stepped behind the women and walked them through the process of holding the clay between their hands and forming it into a ball. She taught them how to use water to moisten the clay.

Olivia looked up from the camera and admired the studio, their classroom, Adira in her element.

Adira glowed with passion and pride. "How about you put that camera down for a little while and take a turn?"

Olivia stopped recording and put the camera back in her bag.

She stepped toward Adira. "Where should I sit?"

"Here. Take my wheel. I'll show you."

The stool, warm on her legs, shook as she put her foot on the pedal.

"You're a natural," Adira said.

Haisley, Paige, and Jara joked with each other and experimented with different shapes. "I think I'm more of a sculptor," Haisley said, pulling off a piece of clay and forming it into a tiny, stick figure goat.

"I think I'm getting the hang of this," said Jara. In front of her was a mass of clay in the shape of a cloud.

"Good thing you came up with that stellar ending and won, Jara. Clay isn't your forte," Haisley joked.

"It's actually pretty fun, though," Jara said. "Relaxing."

Adira moved to the space at Olivia's back. "Is it okay if I show you?"

Olivia nodded, letting Adira wrap her arms around her. Their hands pressed together; Adira guided the clay until it formed into the shape of a bowl.

From Olivia's camera bag, her phone dinged. She thought there might be a new email, and she let it float away like a drifting cloud.

Whatever it is, it can wait.

Maybe this was the decade when she would become un-poke-able, unaffected by the dings and pings of other people's needs and expectations. She could see now that her dreams were somewhere else.

Clay spinning on the wheel, Adira's warmth pressed against the smooth surface of her back, the wind cool and easy blowing through the backyard, the smell of apples and firewood lingering in the air. Olivia smiled.

At last, alive.

ACKNOWLEDGMENTS

First, thank you to every teacher and coach who saw me, heard me, and checked in with me on a personal level. You changed my life. Professor Reed, thank you for inspiring me to pay more attention to stories first told in literature and then through film.

Thank you to my family. Mom, Janelle, Juli, Davey, and Jim. Grandma and Papa. Aunts and uncles. Art, DeLynn, and the rest of the Brainerd family. I love you.

Thank you, Dad, for your support and our conversations over the years, for making sure I got a good education, and for always believing in me.

Inexpressible gratitude to everyone who read and gave feedback on this book along the way. To my writing critique group: Carol, Susan, Donica, and Liz. To my fantastic beta readers: Vickie, Christina R., Christina G., Gloria, Annie, and Rachel. Thank you for your attention to detail, enthusiasm, and gentleness. Greg, Tim, and Stephen, thank you for allowing me to interview you as I learned more about the film industry. My first reader and developmental editor, Cassandra, thank you for your honesty and encouragement. And to Kaity, my second editor, thank you for believing in this book and for finding the spots where it could be better.

Thank you to the entire team at Book Creators and New Degree Press, starting with Eric Koester. Thank you for making this dream possible. Thank you, Haley, Emily, and the rest of the author coaches. And Sharon, thank you for making sure I knew this opportunity existed.

To my fellow book creators, Brittany, Melissa, Arjina, Vickie, Carmen Maria, Sharon, Rebecca, and everyone else. Thank you for your friendship and support.

To my friends, my team, thank you for always being a phone call away.

A *huge* thank you to my partner, Rachel, for delicious meals, steadfast support, and incredible teamwork. I couldn't have done this without you. I love you.

In loving memory of my Nanee, Karen Lineen Welsh, who passed away from COVID-19 in May 2020. Memories of you kept me going when I wanted to quit.

And to everyone who backed this book in various ways, I am forever grateful for your support:

Abby Wagner Stubbs	Adam Johnson
Alexis Rosenblatt	Allison Balter
Allison Jordan	Amanda Hellyar

Amanda Leonesio
Anabell Deutschlander
Arjina Khanom
Ashley Bastow
Blair Academy English Department
Brittany Giannone
Carly Kaskel
Carol and Jim Gildea
Caroline Dosky
Chris Smith
Christina and Brian Radley
CJ Crowder
David Welsh
Diana Niemas
Elisa and Max Adelman
Eliza Davis
Emilee Kadriaj
Emily Brainerd and Peach
Eric Koester
Evelyn Tilney
Gloria Matthews
Halimah Barnett
Hanna McPheron
Helen McDonald
Izzy Hastie
James Moore
Jan Curley Welsh
Jeanie Duncan
Jen Hykes Willson
Jessica Voveris

Amanda Souliotis
Andrew D Sykes
Arthur and DeLynn Brainerd
Bethany Hickey
Brian King
Brittany Wilson
Carmen Maria Navarro
Carol Yee
Chessye Moseley
Christina Gadde
Christine and Bob Curley
Dan Sheedy
Desiree Ficula
Donica Merhazion
Elise Bartosik-Velez
Ellen Hultgren
Emily Bonfiglio
Emily Potz
Eva Centeno
Gina Erickson
Haley Newlin
Hana Merkle Moore
Hannah McCollester
Ilene Cervantes
Jailyn Parnell
Jamie Boutilier
Janelle Welsh
Jeanne Godfroy
Jeremy Scheiner
Jonathan Slawson

Joseph and Dianne Curley
Josh Lauren
Joyce Lang
Julian Serrao
Julie O'Neil
Kat and Steve Nelson
Katie Bale
Kayla Lambright
Kerri Brown
Kristina Kiefer
Kwame Webster
Lauren Bartleson
Laurie Ballantyne Curtis
Lindsey J. Mayer
Liz Kauffman
LW Ray
Mark Wilcox
Masha Stine
Melissa Ann Kerwin O'Neil
Molly Dearing
Monisha Berkowski, PhD
Nakia Hall
Natalia Cerain
Nina Kuzniak
Penn Lunger
Rebecca Garner
Rob May
Robin Greatrex
Samantha Curtis
Sarah Baver

Josh Biber
Joy Lentz
Julia Beaufait
Julianne, Joe, Ella and Jackson Morse
Kadi and Steve Buckley
Kate Sykes
Katrina Turner
Kendra Salvador
Kevin Waters
Kristina Luna
Laura Hayes
Lauren Ricciardi
Leah Brainerd
Lisa Moynihan
Louise and Murray Hood
Mark Simon
Mary Baker
Maureen Curley-Dawson
Michelle Buckley
Molly Maturo
Morning Bugle Productions
Nancy Bisceglia
Nicholas Ansell
Patricia D. Haines
Rachel Brainerd
Rebecca Sela
Rob Strain and Dan Bering
Ryan Pagotto
Sara Bennett
Sarah Pawlak

Shannon MacRoberts	Sharon Podobnik Peterson
Shelli Holland-Handy	Shelly E. Rustek Esten
Shirley McElhaney	Tala el-fahmawi
Tara Sumrall	Thomas Burkett
Vickie Adams	Vickie Savolidis
Weber Gaowen	

CPSIA information can be obtained
at www.ICGtesting.com
Printed in the USA
BVHW030220130622
639643BV00022B/393